The Agile Manager's Guide To

UNDERSTANDING
FINANCIAL STATEMENTS

The Agile Manager's Guide To

UNDERSTANDING
FINANCIAL STATEMENTS

By Joseph T. Straub

Velocity Business Publishing
Bristol, Vermont USA

For Pat and Stacey

Velocity Business Publishing publishes authoritative works of the highest quality. It is not, however, in the business of offering professional, legal, or accounting advice. Each company has its own circumstances and needs, and state and national laws may differ with respect to issues affecting you. If you need legal or other advice pertaining to your situation, secure the services of a professional.

If you'd like additional copies of this book or a catalog of books in the Agile Manager Series®, please get in touch.

- **Write us:**
  Velocity Business Publishing, Inc.
  15 Main Street
  Bristol, VT 05443 USA
- **Call us:**
  1-888-805-8600 in North America (toll-free)
  1-802-453-6669 from all other countries
- **Fax us:**
  1-802-453-2164
- **E-mail us:**
  action@agilemanager.com
- **Visit our Web site:**
  www.agilemanager.com

The Web site contains much of interest to business people—tips and techniques, courses, books for handheld devices, and instant downloads of titles in the Agile Manager Series.

Contents

Books in the Agile Manager Series®:

Introduction

It happens.

You're at a meeting, and the boss looks right at you and says, "What's the ROI on that product again?"

You gulp, trying desperately to remember what "ROI" means. You search your mind for the "R." Revenue? Ratio? Return? You have no idea. Rats. Turning red, you mumble, "Gee, I don't know offhand. I can get back to you, though."

The boss stares at you a few seconds before changing the subject. He doesn't even have to say it out loud: "I expect you to know these things."

Or you're in a job interview, and the interviewer is testing your facility with numbers. "The job requires a passing ability to make sense of the department's finances. Nothing too difficult. Take a look at these for a few minutes," she says, shoving what appear to be financial statements in front of you. "When you're ready, tell me what the debt-to-equity ratio is. And while you're at it, the current ratio and return on equity." She gives you a quick smile, as if it were the easiest thing in the world to pull those figures off the papers in front of you.

7

Actually, coming up with those figures is one of the easier things to do in the business world. Once you become acquainted with such things as the income statement and balance sheet, the numbers leap off the page at you.

The Agile Manager's Guide to Understanding Financial Statements is your guide. You'll learn what the most-used financial statements are and what they tell you. You'll learn useful ratios that will enable you to analyze your operations and improve them. You'll learn how to assess the financial health of your company, an important skill as companies come and go faster than ever. And you'll attract the notice of higher-ups, who tend to promote those who understand the profit motive and use the language of numbers.

Best of all, you'll acquire peace of mind. You'll see that numbers aren't scary things, that they're simply another language that sheds light on business operations. And that speaking in the language of numbers is none too difficult to learn.

You can read *Understanding Financial Statements* in one or two sittings, then refer to it again and again as you need to. The contents, glossary, and index—and the "Best Tips" and "Agile Manager's Checklist" boxes—make it easy to find what you're looking for.

In short, *The Agile Manager's Guide to Understanding Financial Statements* will help you get maximum benefits in your job and career with the least amount of effort.

Chapter One

Financial Statements: Who Needs Them

"I don't know. It's a mysterious thing."

ROGER SMITH, FORMER GENERAL MOTORS CHAIRMAN (WHEN ASKED
BY FORTUNE TO EXPLAIN THE CAUSE OF GM'S FINANCIAL WOES)

"Here you go, partner," said the Agile Manager to Steve, his assistant, as a he threw a small stack of stapled sheets on the desk. Steve looked up quizzically. *"The quarterlies. There's a note for you on top."*

"The quarterly whats?" asked Steve as he looked down and saw rows of numbers on the top page.

"Our quarterly financial statements," responded the Agile Manager. He had meant only to toss them on the desk as he strode by, but now he laid his clipboard down and leaned toward Steve. *"I need you to calculate a few ratios for me before Wednesday's department meeting."*

Steve's heart began to pound and his face turned red. The Agile Manager noticed and said, *"What's the big deal? You have an MBA, right?"*

"Who told you that? I was an English major."

The Agile Manager's jaw dropped slightly. He'd inherited Steve from his predecessor, and he couldn't be happier with Steve's organizational skills and business sense, especially his insight into markets and the psychology buyers bring to it. "You're kidding," he said.

"No." Steve didn't know whether to laugh or remain stone-faced.

"So what do you know about financial statements?"

"Nothing. And I'm scared to death of numbers," he added. "I don't seem to understand them." And he thought, I'm even more afraid of people finding that out . . .

"Good!" said the Agile Manager, brightening. "Together we'll face that fear and you'll be a better man because of it. And more useful to me. We start tomorrow at 9:00 A.M."

After the Agile Manager left, Steve was glum. He thought, Why me? You don't need financial statements to understand business, anyway. Or do you?

Who needs financial statements? You, for starters, and for a number of good reasons. But we'll get back to that in a moment. Plenty of other parties have a keen interest in what these odd documents have to say, so let's get them out of the way now. We'll save the best—what's in it for you—for last.

Several groups of people have a vested interest in a company's financial statements. They include:

1. Management. Financial statements show the essence of management's competence and the sum total (pun intended) of its success. Top managers may be able to hide behind the tinted windows of stretch limos and armies of flunkies and assistants, but the results of their decisions—and whether they've made or lost money for the company—will show up on its financial statements. They can run from the numbers, but they can't hide.

2. Stockholders. Ever bought stock in a company because the CEO dressed nicely or its products claimed to improve your sex life? Probably not. More than likely, you bought stock because the company had a history of solid financial performance. Or, if it was a new business, because you or your stockbroker believed it would make some serious money down the road.

How could you tell? By what it reported on its financial statements, of course. They reveal both past performance and future potential. (And as Charlie Brown once observed, "There's no heavier burden than a great potential.") So we invest in the possibilities that we uncover on the statements and bail out when the statements signal inept management or a dim future. The former usually precedes the latter.

Stockholders who don't understand financial statements end up relying solely on a stockbroker's advice. That puts them at a disadvantage. They don't understand what the broker is talking about, they can't interpret the company's annual report (although the photographs probably look pretty), and they can't ask intelligent questions and make informed decisions about whether to buy or sell. (One clue to corporate trouble anyone can understand: The worse shape a business is in, the more flashy its annual report usually looks.)

3. Present and potential creditors. These include bondholders, suppliers, commercial banks that may give the company a line of credit, landlords, and anyone else the company might end up owing money to.

Best Tip
When you can read financial statements, you won't be totally dependent on the advice of stockbrokers or your department's bean counter.

Creditors that have loaned money to a company with one foot in the grave, or sold stuff to it on account, usually won't throw good money after bad. They'll ask to see financial statements if they suspect trouble. If they're really nervous, they may also demand more collateral (security) for the loans they've made already.

One creditor reportedly made quite an exception for real-estate developer Donald Trump, though.

Back when The Donald was in a bit of a bind, his chief number-cruncher managed to convince a major bank that had loaned him money to pay the six-figure insurance premiums on the *Trump Princess,* a yacht. Trump's minion argued that Donald couldn't afford 'em, and if the insurance lapsed and the yacht were destroyed, the bank would lose a major chunk of collateral. So wouldn't it be smart to pay the insurance? The bank did. (Note: Trump is a professional. Don't try this technique yourself.)

Potential creditors want to verify that the business is in good shape and evaluate how much debt it can safely shoulder before they commit themselves. After they've made the loan or given the company an open-book account, they'll demand, naturally, to see future financial statements to confirm that the company is staying afloat.

How important is it to be able to read financial statements? Consider this. A graduate student who was working on his master's degree in accounting was sent out by a professor to help a panicky small-business owner who was about to go belly-up. The guy's suppliers had cut off his credit the day they saw his latest balance sheet. He had no idea why.

The student looked at the balance sheet (something you'll learn about in chapter three) and discovered a terrible mistake. The CPA who prepared the statement for the naive owner had mistakenly classified the company's $200,000 mortgage balance—which had twenty years to run—as a current liability. That meant it had to be paid within a year. When the suppliers saw this enormous debt supposedly due within the next twelve months, they cut off the company's credit in a New York minute.

When the student confronted the errant CPA with his mistake, he harrumphed, muttered, and briskly ushered the lad out of the office.

The problem was eventually straightened out, and the badly shaken entrepreneur learned a valuable lesson: Owners need to know enough about their companies' statements to read them critically and understand what they're reading, because creditors sure do.

4. Unions. Before contract negotiations come around, unions analyze a company's financial statements to find evidence of poor management, mismanagement, good management, and anything else that might be used as levers in the bargaining process. (Top executives' salaries inevitably take a hit, but the size of their bank accounts cushions the blow.)

Financial-statement information sometimes shows union representatives where management might find money to pay higher wages and/or better benefits, so you can bet your bottom line that a union's financial wizards really take the statements apart. And those guys don't wear hard hats, carry lunch pails, and play touch football. They wear suits, carry laptop computers, and play hardball (around the bargaining table).

Best Tip

Owners: Don't rely solely on your accountant to paint a picture of your company's financial condition.

5. Government. Laws and regulations require companies to report various financial information to several levels of government and associated agencies and bureaus. It's a necessary evil if you want to stay in business. Certain taxes are based on the value of what a company owns, too. And then there's our friend the Internal Revenue Service. Enough said?

What's in It for You

Why should *you* care about financial statements? Because you probably enjoy eating and living indoors. But more specifically:

■ You can relieve your anxiety about your company going bankrupt (or bail out early) by reading its statements. You can also track its financial performance, which has a major impact on the value of your stock options, 401(k) plans, profit-sharing programs, and how much expensive art work top management can buy to decorate the executive suite.

Statements also confirm whether all that downsizing really made as much difference in the company's performance as the boss promised it would.

- You'll learn to make and defend your proposals in dollars and cents. Ditto requests for more and better equipment to run your department, division, or team. And those proposals, no matter what management level you're on, will all have some bearing on your company's financial health.

- You'll learn to speak a new language. Higher management's goals are usually expressed in dollars, and they're relayed down the ladder to the rank and file. That's why accounting has been called "the language of business." Agile managers must be reasonably fluent in it.

|Best Tip

When you learn to speak in the language of numbers, you'll be speaking the language senior managers know and like best.

- You'll understand financial statements and their own peculiar (but not awfully difficult) jargon. That helps you communicate at a higher, more professional level.

This ability tends to level the playing field when you have to communicate with full-time number-crunchers and bean counters who may otherwise try to dazzle you with footwork. A working knowledge of their vocabulary insulates you from being snowed by it and may even help you start a blizzard or two of your own.

- You'll improve your reputation. Speaking in financial terms when the occasion calls for it gives you a reputation as a "bottom line" manager, which higher managers will warm to like a cold dog to a hot stove.

- You'll be prepared to analyze, interpret, and challenge some of the numbers that peers and superiors toss around (especially when they think they can monopolize the meeting).

- You can compare past, present, and projected financial statements from internal profit centers, track important changes from one financial period to the next, and be ready to supply reasons for those changes before someone tries to skewer you across a conference table.

■ You can contrast your company's operations with outside "benchmark" organizations. That can clarify your relative performance and the reasons behind it. You can also compare your own area (department, division, or whatever) with other internal areas, assuming you're all set up as profit centers that make and sell some product or service.

■ You'll be able to evaluate the financial fitness of another company that makes you an attractive job offer—an offer that may not look so great once you've scrutinized the business's finances. Who wants to sign on to rearrange deck chairs on the *Titanic*?

■ Finally, if you understand what financial statements tell you, you can rule out one more thing that your esteemed colleagues might blindside you with when you're jousting for promotions and raises. People don't mess with those who understand numbers. Agile managers uncomplicate their lives as much as possible because they *learn* as much as possible. And that helps them scale that organization chart faster than a lizard up a palm tree.

The Agile Manager's Checklist

✔ You need to understand financial statements to:

  ▪ Analyze the ability of customers to pay you back;
  ▪ Assess the ability of your organization to stay afloat;
  ▪ Defend your proposals to higher management;
  ▪ Gain a reputation as a "bottom line" manager.

✔ Use financial statements to compare your operations with those of competitors or benchmark organizations.

✔ Understand numbers. You'll climb the ladder faster.

Chapter Two

Understand
The Income Statement

"There was an accountant named Wayne
Whose theories were somewhat insane
With sales in recession
He felt an obsession
To prove that a loss was a gain."

ANONYMOUS

It was just before 9:00 A.M. As the Agile Manager waited for Steve to show up, his mind wandered back to a college accounting class in which a graduate student did most of the teaching.

During a grueling question-and-answer session, the teacher had said, "What are you, a bunch of morons? If you can't understand cost of goods sold, I can't wait until you get to inventory valuation."

A friend of the Agile Manager's spoke up: "You make it seem like this stuff is logical. It's not. When you're buying components for a product you're making, why shouldn't you be able to deduct the cost from your revenues right away instead of waiting until the product gets sold?"

17

"Because," sputtered the graduate assistant, "that's the way it is. You can't deduct it until it's sold."

"Yeah," said another student looking at the questioner. "Didn't you know that Moses came down off the mountain with the Generally Accepted Accounting Principles?"

As the class exploded in laughter, the graduate student shook his head and walked out.

It was then that the Agile Manager realized that financial statements were made up of a lot more than numbers. They were also made up of tradition, archaic policy, law, and idiosyncrasies. Knowing that somehow made understanding them easier.

What's an income statement? Glad you asked. It's an accounting statement that summarizes a company's sales, the cost of goods sold, expenses, and profit or loss (plus a few other items thrown in for good measure). Although it's often called a "consolidated earnings statement," plain folks usually call it an income statement.

What the Income Statement Covers

The income statement covers a particular period of time. A company always publishes an annual income statement as part of its yearly report to stockholders. That report also contains two other statements, the balance sheet and statement of cash flows. (We'll get to those in chapters three and four.)

Companies also produce income statements for shorter periods, such as a month or a quarter. They send quarterly statements to stockholders to update them about the company's performance between annual reports.

Quarterly statements are important because they permit management to stay on top of things. If a company produced an income statement only once a year, it could get into a financial jam—and not know until it was too late.

What an Income Statement Shows

When you look at an income statement you'll see:
- Net sales

■ The cost of the goods that were sold. This information shows up on income statements for manufacturing, wholesaling, and retailing firms, because they buy stuff to resell at a profit. A company that provides only services (consulting, financial planning, or writing computer code, for example) wouldn't have a cost of goods sold item on its income statement.

■ Gross profit (Net sales − cost of goods sold = gross profit)

■ Operating expenses (what management spent to run the company during the period that the income statement covers)

■ Earnings before income tax

■ Income tax

■ Net income (if you're lucky or good, or both)

■ Earnings per share of common stock

The skeleton of an income statement, then, looks like this:

> Net Sales
> − Cost of goods sold
> Gross profit
> − Operating expenses
> Earnings before income tax
> − Income tax
> = Net income or (Net loss)
> ... and earnings per share of common stock.

Net income is the fabled "bottom line" that you hear mentioned so often (as in, "What's the bottom line on your proposal to replace all our employees with computers, Smedley?").

Needed: Lots More Detail

Management and the other interested parties that you read about in chapter one (including you) need lots more detail than this skeleton shows.

Figure 2-1 on page 22 shows a fictitious income statement for a company we'll call Avaricious Industries. It's a modest little firm that, if it lives up to its mission statement, hopes to control every aspect of your life someday.

To create a detailed income statement, useful for internal reporting and control, A.I.'s accounting department and management information systems would compile detailed information in categories like:

- Gross sales, sales returns and allowances, and sales discounts that went to produce net sales.
- Information about the methods that were used to value inventory and calculate depreciation on machinery and equipment.
- Individual balances for each of the selling and general-and-administrative expense accounts. Management needs to track the changes in each account from one period to the next and decide whether a particular expense is getting out of control or if the company should spend more money to meet marketing challenges from competitors.

A.I.'s income statement as shown here is relatively simple for a company its size. It would also have a version for internal use that lists every expense account and greater detail in areas like cost of goods sold.

A Word About Accounting Jargon

When it comes to jargon, accounting—like data processing, law, and other highly specialized areas—has its own. Pity. You have to get used to the fact that several different terms mean the same thing or refer to the same idea. This can drive you nuts unless you've been forewarned.

So, while not putting too fine a point on it:

- Revenue and sales are used synonymously. Accountants may prefer "revenue" because it sounds more impressive and helps them defend billing $125 an hour.
- Profit, net income, and earnings all refer to how much money the company made.

- Inventory, merchandise, and goods all mean about the same thing: stuff the company bought and intends to sell to customers for a profit.

- When accountants speak casually (an event so moving that it merits immortalization in a Normal Rockwell print), they may call an income statement a "profit and loss" or "P&L" statement. That's because it indeed shows whether the company made a profit or a loss.

Best Tip

Don't look for detail on an income statement. Account balances are often condensed and summarized.

- Lists or summaries of things like expenses or equipment are typically referred to as "statements" or "schedules." Just don't try to read one to find out when the next bus runs.

- Accountants never just "do" or "make out" these statements or schedules. Heavens, no. They *prepare* them. It sounds much more dignified, mystical, and professional—and beyond the reach of mere mortals. And they never charge you money. They have *fees* for which they send "statements for services rendered." All these discreet euphemisms sound genteel and politically correct, but it's easy to see past the smoke screen.

A Closer Look

So much for an overall view. Climb up on your stool, don your green eyeshade, and let's have a close-up look at Figure 2-1.

Net sales (or revenue). As mentioned, this is what was really sold after customers' returns, sales discounts, and other allowances were taken away from gross sales. Companies usually just show the net sales amount on their income statements and don't bother to show returns, allowances, and the like.

Cost of goods sold. This usually appears as one amount on an annual report, but it takes a little figuring to come up with. Let's see how we arrived at the numbers by taking a closer look:

Figure 2-1

Avaricious Industries
Consolidated Earnings Statement
For Year Ended December 31, 19XX

Net sales		$38,028,500
Cost of goods sold:		
Inventory, January 1	4,190,000	
Purchases (net)	25,418,500	
Goods available for sale	29,608,500	
Less inventory, December 31	3,250,000	
Cost of goods sold:		26,358,500
Gross profit		11,670,000
Operating expenses		
Selling:		
Sales salaries expense	1,991,360	
Advertising expense	3,527,650	
Sales promotion expense	987,745	
Depreciation expense—		
selling equipment	403,850	6,910,605
General and administrative:		
Office salaries expense	1,124,650	
Repairs expense	112,655	
Utilities expense	39,700	
Insurance expense	48,780	
Equipment expense	63,750	
Interest expense	211,020	
Misc. expenses	650,100	
Depreciation expense—		
office equipment	73,900	2,324,555
Total operating expenses		9,235,160
Earnings before income tax		2,434,840
Income tax		925,239
Net income		$1,509,601
Common stock shares outstanding:		2,500,000
Earnings per share of common stock:		$0.60

Inventory, January 1	$4,190,000
Purchases (net)	25,418,500
Goods available for sale	29,608,500
Less inventory, December 31	3,250,000
Cost of goods sold:	$26,358,500

The January 1 inventory was the goods that Avaricious started the year with, but the company bought lots more to resell during the year. Again, details such as purchases returns and allowances may be omitted, so just the net amount of purchases shows up on the statement.

New purchases are added to the beginning inventory to get the dollar amount of goods available for sale. That's what the company paid for everything it could have sold this year if it were down to the bare shelves. But it's not; it has an inventory of goods still on the shelves on December 31. When that ending inventory is subtracted from goods available for sale, Bingo! You've got the cost of goods sold.

Note: Avaricious Industries is—for now—a distributor. It buys finished goods and resells them to retail stores and individuals. But Avaricious hopes one day to live up to its name and actually make things. When that happens, its cost of goods sold will be made up of purchases of raw materials, finished components, and a bunch of other things like the labor that goes into producing what it makes.

Gross profit. How much the company made before expenses and taxes are taken away.

Operating expenses. This section of the income statement adds up how much money was spent to run the company this year.

Selling expenses include everything spent to run the sales end of the business, like sales salaries, travel, meals and lodging for salespeople, and advertising.

General-and-administrative expenses are the total amount spent to run the non-sales part of the company. These expenses include rent, office salaries, interest on loans, depreciation, and any other non-sales expenses such as renting stretch limos and chauffeurs for top managers.

Earnings before income tax. This is the profit the company made before income taxes (sob).

Income tax. What the company had better have paid the IRS if it wants to stay in business.

Net income. (Bet you thought we'd never get here.) This is the profit the company made after all the dust clears. If the business *lost* money (a thought that makes accountants break out in hives), this line would be labeled "Net loss," and several scapegoat middle managers would probably be flogged publicly in front of the fountain at corporate headquarters.

Earnings per share of common stock. You'll find out more

Read the notes in an annual report. That's where the bodies are buried.

about this item when we get to financial analysis and start uncovering hidden information on the statements. For now, let's just divide the net income by the number of shares of common stock the company has sold (shares "outstanding").

The higher earnings per share are, the more spectacular job management is doing running "your" company—if you own shares. (Just don't ask to borrow that stretch limo for the weekend. Your picture will show up in the executive dining room as "Moron Stockholder of the Month.")

A Note About Notes

Every annual report has several pages of notes at the end. These discuss finer points about its operations and accounting techniques.

Such notes would explain which methods were applied to calculate certain items, the Generally Accepted Accounting Principles (GAAP) followed, and a variety of other arcane information that may contain some real eye-opening facts if you can read them without falling asleep. Good luck!

For example:

1. Notes might point out that 20 percent of this year's sales are the proceeds from selling off one of the Picasso paintings in the boardroom. Such one-shot deals/isolated or unusual transactions may make the company's financial condition look better or worse than it normally would.

2. Notes may also reveal information about lease contracts for facilities or office equipment (which may require payments of several million dollars a year) that the company has agreed to pay for the next few years. This information may have a major impact on future profits if sales decline or the annual payments are scheduled to escalate.

3. Notes should disclose if the company has been named as a defendant in any product-liability, environmental-pollution, antitrust, or patent-infringement lawsuits. They should also discuss its likely "exposure" (how much of its shirt the company may lose, including attorneys' fees) if the other side wins. In these cases, the notes should also discuss what amount of the potential loss is covered by insurance and whether losing the case would have a "material adverse affect" (as it's sometimes called) on the company's financial condition.

The Agile Manager's Checklist

✔ An income statement covers a period of time, like a quarter or a year. By subtracting various expenses from sales, it reveals the fabled "bottom line."

✔ "Revenue" and "sales" are synonymous. So are "net income," "profit," and "earnings."

✔ Gross profit is sales minus cost of goods sold. Net profit (or net income) is gross profit minus expenses and taxes.

Chapter Three

Understand The Balance Sheet

"Old accountants never die; they just lose their balance."

The Agile Manager reflected on his lessons with Steve. Days one and two had been a bit rough. It took the first day just to wear down his resistance to numbers in general, and the second day for him to be able to define, acceptably, things like cost of goods sold. He was dreading today's session, in which they'd tackle the balance sheet.

But it went better than he thought. Towards the end of the session, Steve punched a few numbers into a calculator. "So the book value of the company is $24 per share. Equity divided by the number of shares, right?" He looked up. The Agile Manager nodded. "But our stock price is $79. How can that be?"

"Aha! You know the stock price. You can't be too oblivious to numbers." The Agile Manager jabbed Steve in the ribs playfully.

"Of course I do," said Steve. "A good part of my retirement plan is invested in the company's stock."

The Agile Manager said, "Market price is usually higher than book value. That's the way it is with a publicly traded company. In our case, people aren't buying shares in what we have. They are buying shares in what they think we will become in the future—a bigger company with increasing revenues and profits."

"Still," said Steve, "book value bears some relationship to market value, don't you think? If only as a reference point?"

"Yep. And you know what? You're already starting to talk like an old pro . . ."

A balance sheet fleshes out what accountants call the "basic accounting equation":

Assets = Liabilities + Owner's Equity

Each part of this equation can be defined simply:

Assets are anything of value that a company owns, like cash, accounts receivable, inventory, buildings, or equipment.

Liabilities are what the company owes to creditors. In plain language, they're debts. But referring to them as "liabilities" sounds more weighty and profound and helps accountants polish their erudite image as they bill you $100 per hour to interpret this stuff. ("Liabilities? Well, we . . . [ahem] we might think of them as financial obligations of the firm. They're amounts, that is, sums of money, that the company owes to outside parties. I suppose you might call them debts. That'll be $100.")

Owner's equity (or net worth) is the stake or interest that the owners have in the company. In a corporation, owner's equity is called stockholders' equity. If the company is a partnership, it would be partners' equity. If the business is a sole proprietorship (which means it's owned by one guy or gal), owner's equity could also be called capital or net worth. Remember what we said back in

|Best Tip

The balance sheet freezes the company's account balances at a single point in time. The balance sheet can be obsolete the very next day.

chapter two about several accounting terms meaning the same thing? Told ya!

Balance Sheet: Distinguishing Features

What makes a balance sheet different from an income statement? For one thing, it doesn't summarize information for certain accounts as the income statement does.

Rather, a balance sheet is a "snapshot" statement. The company is frozen on the date shown at the top, and the balances in its balance sheet accounts are shown on that specific day— typically the last day of the month or year.

> **|Best Tip**
>
> A service business will most likely not have an inventory of any of value.

Most of the accounts on a balance sheet have at least one thing in common: Their balances fluctuate a little bit every day because of the day's business activities. Also, the balances in a company's balance sheet accounts run perpetually. In contrast, the balances in the income statement accounts (sales, expenses, purchases, and freight, for example) are reset to zero or "closed out" at the beginning of the new financial year.

Figure 3-1 on the following page shows the balance sheet for Avaricious Industries.

Up Close and Personal With a Balance Sheet

Let's carve out the main sections of A.I.'s balance sheet and look at them closer.

Assets. Again, these are anything of value that the company owns. That includes cash, accounts receivable from customers that the business has sold to on credit, the coffee machine that's always breaking down in the break room, and that $2 million Picasso hanging in the CEO's office. Assets are typically broken down into "current assets" and "property and equipment."

Current assets are cash, things that will be converted into cash

Figure 3-1

Avaricious Industries
Balance Sheet
December 31, 19XX

ASSETS

Current assets			
Cash and cash equivalents		$1,271,231	
Accounts receivable	1,032,409		
less allowance for			
doubtful accounts	38,000	994,409	
Notes receivable		350,000	
Merchandise inventories		3,250,000	
Total current assets			5,865,640
Property and equipment		17,841,980	
Less accumulated depreciation		4,173,130	
Net property and equipment			13,668,850
TOTAL ASSETS			$19,534,490

LIABILITIES

Current liabilities			
Accounts payable	1,275,300		
Salaries payable	330,000		
Income taxes payable	925,239		
Other accrued expenses	8,000		
Total current liabilities		2,538,539	
Long-term liabilities			
Mortgage payable	500,000		
Bonds payable	2,400,000		
Total long-term liabilities		2,900,000	
TOTAL LIABILITIES			5,438,539

STOCKHOLDERS' EQUITY

Common stock, 2,500,000 shares			
at $1 par value per share		2,500,000	
Capital in excess of par value		1,750,000	
Retained earnings, January 1	8,386,350		
Net income for year	1,509,601		
Less dividends	(50,000)		
Retained earnings, December 31, 19xx		9,845,951	
TOTAL STOCKHOLDERS' EQUITY			14,095,951
TOTAL LIABILITIES AND			
STOCKHOLDERS' EQUITY			$19,534,490

within a year (such as accounts receivable and the current portion of any notes receivable), and inventory, which turns into cash when it's sold. Keep looking at the asset section of the balance sheet as we investigate these items in detail.

Cash and cash equivalents. This is the balance in the company's checking account(s), plus highly liquid short-term or temporary investments (sometimes called "marketable securities"). These might include certificates of deposit, stocks, and corporate or U.S. government bonds, all investments that the company could probably sell with a telephone call to its bank or brokerage firm. They were initially bought to keep excess cash working instead of leaving it to gather dust in a non-interest-bearing checking account.

Accounts receivable and notes receivable. Accounts receivable are owed to the company by customers to which it sold goods or services on credit. Notes receivable are promissory notes that the company will collect in less than a year. (Notes receivable due in more than a year would be listed as a long-term asset.)

Notice that the total accounts receivable balance is reduced by an allowance for doubtful accounts. That's the accountant's practical side at work, telling you that the business probably won't collect *all* of those accounts.

In a big business that has literally hundreds if not thousands of credit customers, some will inevitably turn out to be deadbeats or go bankrupt. So the accountants estimate what percentage of the company's receivables will turn sour and subtract that amount. The result is a realistic net amount that the company expects (crossing its fingers) to collect.

Merchandise inventories. If the company is a retailing or wholesaling business, this is the value of products that the company has bought and intends to resell for a profit. In a manufacturing business, inventories include finished goods that are sitting in the warehouse as well as goods in process (those in various stages of completion), raw materials, and parts and components that will go into the end product.

You can calculate the value of a company's inventory using one of four methods. Sit tight; there'll be more about this in chapter six.

The second category of assets, property and equipment, are, well, property and equipment. The business uses them to make the product or provide the service that it sells.

Land, buildings, machinery, and equipment fall under this heading. They're shown at the cost the company paid to buy or build them (including such expenses as installation costs and taxes) minus the amount that they've depreciated since they were bought or built.

Best Tip
Liabilities and stockholders' equity represent claims against a company's assets. That's why the balance sheet balances.

Depreciation can be plain old wear-and-tear, technological obsolescence—the kind that makes the computer you paid $3,500 for last year worth $800 today—or both.

Land isn't depreciated, by the way, because you never use it up and they aren't making any more of it. Raw land is shown on the balance sheet at its purchase price and neither appraised nor depreciated as years go by. If the land and the building are eventually sold, the difference between the land's cost and what was received on the sale would be recorded as a gain (if greater than cost) or loss (if less than cost) on sale of plant and equipment.

Some companies may have other categories of assets too, including intangible assets such as patents and copyrights. Current assets and P&E are the two major players, however.

Liabilities. This section, which we'll reproduce here as Figure 3-2 to save you from having to flip back a page, shows all the debts the company owes to creditors of every kind. Even employees are creditors of the company on the balance sheet date, because it owes them salaries that won't be paid until payday.

Current liabilities are bills the company must pay within the next twelve months. Long-term liabilities are bills that will come

---

Figure 3-2

Current Liabilities		
Accounts payable	$1,275,300	
Salaries payable	330,000	
Income taxes payable	925,239	
Other accrued expenses	8,000	
Total current liabilities		2,538,539
Long-term liabilities		
Mortgage payable	500,000	
Bonds payable	2,400,000	
Total long-term liabilities		2,900,000
TOTAL LIABILITIES		**$5,438,539**

---

due in more than one year. As Figure 3-2 shows, A.I. owes $500,000 on a mortgage and $2,400,000 on bonds that it sold to raise funds. Total liabilities? Almost $5.5 million.

Stockholders' Equity. This section shows what the company is worth to its owners—those optimistic, hopeful stockholders, including widows, orphans, and retirees living on Social Security, who risked their life savings to cast their lot with the future of Avaricious Industries.

As Figure 3-3 shows, Avaricious Industries has sold 2,500,000 shares of stock. Management used the money it got from stock sales (along with what it borrowed by issuing bonds) first to start and then expand the business.

You'll notice that A.I.'s stock has a "par value" of $1.00 per share. That's an arbitrary figure that has nothing to do with what

---

Figure 3-3

Common stock, 2,500,000 shares		
at $1 par value per share		2,500,000
Capital in excess of par value		1,750,000
Retained earnings, January 1,	8,386,350	
Net income for year	1,509,601	
Less dividends	(50,000)	
Retained earnings,		
December 31, 19xx		9,845,951
TOTAL STOCKHOLDERS' EQUITY		$14,095,951

the stock is selling for right now on the open market. While it's customary to assign a par value to stock, as A.I. did, the number doesn't have much meaning. It's a relic from the pre-Depression era, when stock had to be sold at its par value.

|B̲e̲s̲t̲ Tip

Don't even try to figure out what relation "par value" has to anything. Accountants have a hard time explaining it!

Securities regulations nonetheless still require par value to be accounted for separately from other types of additional paid-in capital, which is why A.I.'s balance sheet carries an account called "capital in excess of par value." Because A.I. sold some of its stock for more than the $1.00 par value per share, the excess is shown in that account.

Then there are retained earnings, the profits A.I.'s management has plowed back into the business over the years. Last January's retained earnings, plus the net income or profit that the company made this year (which is carried over here from the income statement), minus dividends, equals the retained earnings on the balance sheet date of December 31. And when you add in the par value of its common stock and the capital received in excess of par, you have the total stockholders' equity.

A Balancing Act

As Figure 3-1 shows, the balance sheet really does balance. That is, A.I.'s total assets equal the sum of the creditors' claims against them (liabilities) and the stockholders' claims against them (the owners' or stockholders' equity). The balance sheet, in fact, always balances, even when liabilities exceed assets. In that case, equity is a negative number—and the company is dead or close to it, barring an infusion of capital.

Theoretically, if Avaricious Industries were sold today, the sale would bring in $19,534,490. Creditors would be paid $5,438,539 to take a hike, and the stockholders would divvy up the remaining $14,095,951 (or $5.64 per share) among themselves.

Theory and reality are two different things, however, so the sale could bring in quite a bit more money—or quite a bit less. A selling price depends on the industry, long-term profitability, the company's prospects, and a host of other concerns to buyers.

The Agile Manager's Checklist

✔ A balance sheet is a one-day "snapshot" of the company's assets, debts, and owners' equity.

✔ A balance sheet shows assets (what the company owns) and sets them equal to its liabilities (what the company owes) plus the owners' equity in the business.

✔ Theoretically, stockholders' equity is what the stockholders would collect if the company were sold on the balance sheet date.

✔ Retained earnings on December 31 is last year's retained earnings plus this year's net income.

Chapter Four

Understand The Cash-Flow Statement

"If your outgo exceeds your inflow, then your upkeep will be your downfall."

ANONYMOUS

"Now we're getting into it, Stevie," said the Agile Manager rubbing his hands together. "Cash flow is what it's all about. If cash flow is healthy, it covers a lot of sins."

"I don't get it. Doesn't every company have a lot of cash flowing in and out of it?"

"Yeah, but cash flow usually refers to the excess of cash coming in over the cash going out. It means you have cash in the bank to pay bills, fund initiatives, sock a little away for a rainy day, and so on—no matter what your income statement says about your profits." The Agile Manager leaned back.

"I once worked for a company that didn't make a profit five years in a row," he said. "But the owner never missed her yearly trip to Bermuda, and she leased a Benz every two years. And we were all paid well and had good equipment to work with."

"But how'd she do it?" Steve interjected excitedly.

"Great cash flow. She was absolutely brilliant at timing income with outflow. When one product was selling great, she'd shovel the cash into R&D and product development. When nothing was happening, she'd lay low for a while and cut back on expenses. She also had a pretty sharp accountant who knew how to spread losses around, as well as a few other tricks—all legal—for reducing the profit."

"But isn't profit good?"

"It's necessary, especially for publicly held companies. But profit is one of those things that can be manipulated up or down. And sole owners tend to like it down, so they don't have to pay taxes on it." He straightened up again.

"Your cash flow, however, never lies. Let me show you what I mean . . ."

A cash-flow statement shows where the company's cash came from (sources of cash) and where it went (uses of cash). Like an income statement, the cash-flow statement covers a block of time, such as a month or year. Avaricious Industries' cash-flow statement appears in Figure 4-1 on the following page.

As you'll see, net income is only the starting point for figuring out actual cash on hand at the end of the year.

Best Tip

The income statement and balance sheet don't tell you as much as you need to know about your financial position.

Cash Flow: It's a Big Deal

As our whimsical opening quote implies, a company's cash flow deserves plenty of attention. There are cases of companies that had millions of dollars in noncash assets—and profitability on paper—but which had to close down because they couldn't keep enough cash on hand to pay their regular monthly bills and run the company day to day.

Figure 4-1

Avaricious Industries
Cash Flow Statement
For Year Ended December 31, 19XX

Cash flows from operations:		
Net income		$1,509,601
Adjustments to reconcile net income to net cash		
Increase in accounts receivable	(221,275)	
Decrease in inventories	940,000	
Increase in notes receivable	(30,000)	
Decrease in accounts payable	(202,500)	
Depreciation on equipment	477,750	
Net cash provided by operations		2,473,576
Cash flows from investing activities		
Purchase of property and equipment	(2,080,695)	
Proceeds from sale of equipment	160,000	
Net cash used for investing activities		(1,920,695)
Cash flows from financing activities		
Sale of common stock	25,000	
Sale of bonds	65,750	
Cash dividends paid	(50,000)	
Net cash inflow from financing activities		40,750
Net increase (decrease) in cash		593,631
Cash balance, December 31, 19XX (last year)		677,600
Cash balance, December 31, 19XX (this year)		$1,271,231

Businesses, like people, sometimes spend recklessly, anticipate sales from uncertain sources such as landing that "big contract" (the corporate version of winning the lottery), expect rapid payment of accounts receivable (ha), and otherwise live beyond their means.

Businesses sometimes also pay too much attention to their income statements to make decisions. That can be dangerous, because virtually all corporations keep their books on an "accrual" basis. This means they record income when they make the sale, and not when they receive the cash. Similarly, they record expenses when they incur them, not when they pay them. (Recording income when you receive it and expenses when you pay them is called "cash-based" accounting. It's probably how you manage your home finances.)

That's why a company can be profitable on paper, while struggling to come up with the cash to fund growth or pay bills.

What It's Good For

Because a cash-flow statement shows sources and uses of cash, it can be used to:

1. Forecast future cash flows. How? Previous cash receipts and disbursements establish a pattern. Management can use it to predict where cash is most likely to come from and go to next year.

2. Show the company's owners and creditors how much management invested last year in new equipment and facilities. Businesses need to invest in such state-of-the-art technology as CAD/CAM, CIM, robotics, and bar-code inventory tracking systems—not to mention update their existing software and hardware—to stay on the cutting edge of productivity and pare operating costs to the bone. (The slogan of companies that don't upgrade their facilities and equipment might be, "Answering yesterday's challenges tomorrow or the next day.")

Best Tip
Use the cash-flow statement to anticipate cash shortages or excesses—months before they hit.

The cash-flow statement can also be used to confirm whether a company has enough cash available to pay interest to bondholders and dividends to stockholders. If a firm has bonds outstanding, management will have to contribute cash to a sinking fund each year—an account set up specifically to hold money used to pay off both bond interest and principal. (Companies usually invest the money in their sinking funds with the hopes that they can earn returns good enough to retire bonds early.)

Dissecting a Cash-flow Statement

Let's take a look at each part of A.I.'s cash-flow statement to see what happened last year.

Cash flows from operations. This section shows how much cash came into the company and how much went out during the normal course of business. Figure 4-2 below starts with A.I.'s net profit (the "bottom line" of the income statement).

Several other aspects of the company's operations either increased or decreased its cash, however, and those are shown under the "adjustments" heading. Generally Accepted Accounting Principles (GAAPs) as well as logic dictate how these adjustments are made on the cash-flow statement and whether they increased or decreased the company's supply of cash.

While not venturing too far into the technical forest, let's look at the adjustments and their consequences.

A.I.'s ending accounts receivable balance this year (you'll find that on the balance sheet on page 30) was $221,275 higher than last year's, which acted to decrease its cash balance. The logic here: An increase in receivables is money earned and reflected in the net income. But Avaricious doesn't actually have that money yet, hence the decrease in actual cash on hand.

For the same reason, the increase in the notes receivable balance also signals a reduction in cash.

A decrease in accounts payable balance also decreases cash

Figure 4-2		
Cash flows from operations:		
Net income		$1,509,601
Adjustments to reconcile net income to net cash		
Increase in accounts receivable	(221,275)	
Decrease in inventories	940,000	
Increase in notes receivable	(30,000)	
Decrease in accounts payable	(202,500)	
Depreciation on equipment	477,750	
Net cash provided by operations		$2,473,576

because you've used funds to pay down the overall balance in the account.

The company's ending inventory was $940,000 lower than its beginning inventory (you'll find both inventory levels on the income statement on page 22). That acts to free up (increase) cash previously sitting in inventory.

Since depreciation on equipment didn't physically decrease the company's cash balance—it's only an accounting fiction— accounting rules call for it to be shown as an inflow of cash from operations.

Cash flows from investing activities. Cash may come in and go out because of various investing activities that aren't connected to business as usual.

Figure 4-3 shows that A.I.'s management bought more than $2 million worth of property and equipment (which caused cash to go out) and sold some obsolete or unneeded equipment (which brought cash in). The net effect of these investing activities decreased cash about $1.9 million.

The investment in property and equipment is an investment in the company's future; it should enhance its competitive position. (Let's have a round of applause for proactive management!)

And the inflow from equipment sales was minimal, a good sign. Unlike some cash-strapped companies, A.I. hasn't been forced to sell off equipment to cover expenses.

A company that's forced to do that is like a sinking ship that jettisons its cargo to stay afloat. If it survives at all, it'll just be an empty shell that eventually washes up on the rocky shoals of bankruptcy. There it'll be picked clean by beachcombing scavengers such as vultures wearing Armani suits and fiddler crabs

---

Figure 4-3

Cash flows from investing activities		
Purchase of property and equipment	(2,080,695)	
Proceeds from sale of equipment	160,000	
Net cash used for investing activities		($1,920,695)

Figure 4-4

Cash flows from financing activities		
Sale of common stock	25,000	
Sale of bonds	65,750	
Cash dividends paid	(50,000)	
Net cash inflow from financing activities		$40,750

---

wearing tiny little "IRS Swat Team" caps, mirrored sunglasses, and, of course, white socks (required by their government contract).

Cash flows from financing activities. A.I. raised $90,750 in cash by selling common stock and bonds this year (see Figure 4-4). The company also paid out $50,000 in cash dividends to stockholders and ended up with a net cash inflow of $40,750 from financing activities.

As Figure 4-1 shows, A.I. had a net increase in cash this year, and most of its cash came from operations. That's good. Healthy companies are able to meet their normal cash requirements through operations.

Best Tip

A company that has to rely on financing activities (such as selling stock or bonds) to satisfy most of its cash requirements is headed for trouble.

Long-term financing (selling shares of stock or bonds, or getting a multi-year loan) should be used to raise funds for acquiring new machinery, equipment, or facilities—never to pay daily business bills.

A negative cash flow from operations means that the company failed to meet its cash needs. In that case, the company must lower expenses quickly or raise cash. The notes at the end of one small corporation's annual report discreetly revealed that it was so hard up for cash that it had borrowed on the cash surrender value of its life insurance policy on the chief executive officer!

The final entry on A.I.'s cash-flow statement is the ending

cash balance for the year, which is (no surprise) the same as the cash balance on the balance sheet.

The Agile Manager's Checklist

✔ The cash-flow statement reconciles a company's cash balance from one year to the next.

✔ The cash-flow statement shows the net cash flow from:

- Normal operations;
- Investing activities, such as buying new equipment and selling obsolete equipment;
- Financing activities, such as selling stock or bonds and paying out dividends.

✔ While depreciation is deducted on the income statement to come up with net income, it doesn't decrease the company's cash.

✔ Note how much a company invested in its operations. It's a telling figure.

Chapter Five

Financial Analysis: Number-Crunching for Profit

"Just dropped in to see what condition your condition was in."

PARAPHRASE OF LINE FROM A POPULAR 1960s SONG

"Besides return on investment for the products this department produces, I like to look at companywide things like sales per employee and return on net assets," said the Agile Manager.

"Why bother?" said Steve. "Don't we have plenty of bean counters at corporate to worry about stuff like that?"

"I don't care whether we do or not. It's part of my early warning system. Tells me about the overall health of the company. If the sales-per-employee figure is slipping, for example, then I'm careful about requesting funds for a new hire. If the return on assets or equity is declining, I can expect some kind of belt-tightening program. It's not a question of if, but when."

"But how do you know what those numbers mean to the senior managers? How do you know what makes 'em happy or sad?"

"I don't know for sure. But I suspect they're doing what I do: Comparing them to figures for our competitors. Look at this," he said pulling a sheet from the top drawer of his battered desk. "This

45

is a list of common ratios for our industry. It's compiled by the Medical Products Manufacturers Association from real numbers. To be part of the organization, you have to submit financial data."

"Hmm," said Steve thoughtfully as he gazed at the page. "The average sales per employee for a company our size is $322,500. And based on your calculation"—Steve leaned over to glance at the Agile Manager's yellow pad—"we're at around $375,000. Hey—bonus city this year, right?"

"Sure—if it were up to me alone," said the Agile Manager chuckling. "But that figure will benefit you in other ways. I just got the approval to hire another developer, which will take the load off the rest of us. And we'll be getting a new test bench next month . . ."

Most people seem drawn to, indeed, fascinated by, things with beautiful shapes. It's part of our aesthetic, kinder-gentler-art-loving side to want to gaze upon visually appealing objects that speak to and nurture our inner spirit . . . the daring lines of a Dodge Viper, the breathtaking beauty and simplicity of a tulip in May, or the financial statements of a company that outwardly seems so rock-solid that it seems to work out twice a day.

But how can you gently strip away its corporate clothing layer by layer to reveal whether that company is really in great shape or just trying to dazzle you with the business version of a face lift, tummy tuck, Rogaine, or hair transplants?

By reading this chapter, of course!

Liars May Figure, But Figures Don't Lie

Financial analysis is the company version of an annual physical (cough). Sometimes it's called "ratio analysis," although some of the digital checkups we'll do are ratios and some aren't.

Financial analysis can be fun. Don't adjust your glasses; you read that right. Why fun? Because statements conceal lots of important (and sometimes delightful or terrifying) facts just by the way they're laid out. The information isn't all that obvious.

It's not that someone's trying to pull a fast one (usually not, anyway). But eyeballing statements to evaluate a company's condition will only give you eyestrain. They don't connect certain pieces of information the way they'll be connected, related, and explained in plain language here.

You'll notice that we sort of eased up to the topic of a company's financial fitness casually, as if we were approaching the firm in a singles bar. We checked it out in general from a distance by ogling the income statement and balance sheet. Now it's time to make a serious move.

Best Tip

There's no "best" calculation that answers the question, "How's the business doing?"

Take Precautions First

"Precautions" here means there's no one best calculation you can do with a company's financial statements that neatly answers the question, "How's the business doing?" Some of the calculations we'll do may show that it's in great shape. Others may show it's in trouble.

And something else: Most of what you'll find out about our friend Avaricious Industries in this chapter will mean lots more when stacked up against comparative data from a reliable source. "Comparative data" means what's typical for other companies in the same line of business as A.I. "Reliable source" can refer to several possible places:

- The company's trade association, which should be able to summarize the average performance for a company in that particular industry.
- Dun & Bradstreet, which publishes key ratios for more than one hundred lines of business each year.
- Robert Morris Associates' *Annual Statement Studies*, which examines the annual financial statements of lots and lots of companies of all sizes and in all industries. Your library should have a copy. (And business owners: Be aware that your banker will probably check your financial statements against it when you march in to ask for a loan.)

One more tidbit. Remember that what's considered good performance in one industry may be not so good in another. It depends on the nature of the business itself. Retailing businesses, for example, are very different creatures from cement producers, computer manufacturers, or companies that write software. Each group of animals in the business zoo has distinct norms and behavior.

Financial Voyeurism

Think of the calculations you're going to learn about as individual windows you can look through. They are just like the windows in a house. Each gives you a different view of what's going on inside, and some views may be lots more interesting than others. But no one window in a house lets you see everything that's going on inside, just like no one calculation shows you everything that's going on inside a company. You have to do a number of them.

Best Tip
Most of the information that financial analysis uncovers takes on a lot more meaning when you compare it with industry standards.

So let's play Peeping Tom (financially speaking) and see what happens when we peek over A.I.'s corporate window sills. Grab your calculator and come on!

Analyzing an Income Statement

Here we'll hark back to Figure 2-1 and pull off whatever numbers we need. (It's reproduced on the next page.)

Ratio of Net Income to Net Sales. Find this by dividing net income by net sales:

$$\frac{\text{Net income}}{\text{Net sales}} = \frac{\$\ 1,509,601}{\$38,028,500} = \$.04 : \$1$$

This ratio tells you how much net income (or profit) a com-

Avaricious Industries
Consolidated Earnings Statement
For Year Ended December 31, 19XX

Net sales			$38,028,500
Cost of goods sold:			
Inventory, January 1		4,190,000	
Purchases (net)		25,418,500	
Goods available for sale		29,608,500	
Less inventory, December 31		3,250,000	
Cost of goods sold:			26,358,500
Gross profit			11,670,000
Operating expenses			
Selling:			
Sales salaries expense	1,991,360		
Advertising expense	3,527,650		
Sales promotion expense	987,745		
Depreciation expense—			
selling equipment	403,850	6,910,605	
General and administrative:			
Office salaries expense	1,124,650		
Repairs expense	112,655		
Utilities expense	39,700		
Insurance expense	48,780		
Equipment expense	63,750		
Interest expense	211,020		
Misc. expenses	650,100		
Depreciation expense—			
office equipment	73,900	2,324,555	
Total operating expenses			9,235,160
Earnings before income tax			2,434,840
Income tax			925,239
Net income			$1,509,601
Common stock shares outstanding:			2,500,000
Earnings per share of common stock:			$0.60

pany makes on each $1.00 of net sales. A.I. made 4 cents of net income on each dollar it collected in net sales. Is that good or bad? It depends on what's typical for A.I.'s industry.

In the supermarket industry, two to five cents on each dollar of net sales is about average year in and year out. Maybe that's why you see delicatessens, fast-food restaurants, pharmacies, flower shops, bank branches, and plastic surgery salons now appearing inside many of the larger supermarkets near you. Those operations return a higher profit on each dollar of net sales and make up for the grocery business's meager profits. (We're only kidding about the plastic surgery salons, but they're probably in the works. Don't forget where you heard the idea first!)

Chipmaker Intel, on the other hand, has been known to make upwards of 25 cents on each dollar of revenue—now there's an avaricious industry!

Incidentally, the formula above also yields a figure for something you've probably heard of—net profit margin. It's expressed in percentage form. AI's net profit margin is thus 4 percent.

Let's detour here for a moment and use this ratio to make several points about figuring and understanding ratios in general.

- When the ingredients are named in the title (as in "ratio of net income to net sales") put the first item *above* the line and the second one *below*. That's a handy memory key in case you're ever caught without this book (God forbid!).

- Once you've set it up, **Always divide the lower number into the upper one.** (Put another way, always divide the upper number by the lower number.) That's Straub's first law of ratio math. If you do it the other way, you'll be dead wrong, and full-time financial types will sneer as you walk past the water cooler.

- When you get the answer, write it down and put it the form " : $1" because ratios compare one thing to another.

So much for mechanics. Now here's how you interpret any ratio:

—The first number in your answer always refers to whatever was above the line (in this case, net income) and the 1 always refers to whatever's underneath (in this case, net sales).

—Lots of folks like to express ratios in money instead of bland-sounding numbers, because people really tend to listen up whenever money's involved. No surprise, huh? So we'll be talking ratios in money here.

Now, back to the show.

Ratio of Net Sales to Net Income. This flip-flops the two ingredients used above, but you'll still get some useful information. A.I.'s ratio is:

$$\frac{\text{Net sales}}{\text{Net income}} = \frac{\$38,028,500}{\$\ 1,509,601} = \$25.19 : \$1$$

This ratio tells you that A.I. had to take in $25.19 in net sales to make a dollar of profit. That's how hard the company has to work to make a buck.

So if $1.00 out of every $25.19 of net sales ended up as net income, where did the other $24.19 go? Well, some went to cover the cost of the goods that were sold, and the rest went to pay expenses.

Remember now, don't jump to conclusions about any of this information until you get a comparative figure from a reliable source. What looks good for a company in one industry may be not so good for a company in a different line of business. Once you found out what the typical ratio of net income to net sales was for A.I.'s industry, though, you'd know if Avaricious had to work harder or easier than its typical competitor to make a dollar of profit.

Inventory Turnover. This is a theoretical figure. It's the number of times the company sold out to the bare walls and replaced its average stock of goods this year. A.I.'s inventory turnover is:

$$\frac{\text{Cost of goods sold}}{\text{Average inventory (beginning inventory + ending)/2}}$$

$$\frac{\$26,358,500}{(\$4,190,000 + \$3,250,000)/2} = 7.09 \text{ times}$$

Note that inventory turnover isn't expressed as a ratio, percent, or some other way. You'd simply say that A.I. turned over its average stock of goods 7.09 *times* this year.

A "good" turnover figure depends on what line of business you're in. Jewelry stores, for example, may be lucky to turn over (sell out) their average inventory once a year. Supermarkets and health-food stores, which sell perishable items, turn over their inventory dozens of times in a year. Get a comparative figure for your line of business.

What if turnover's low? A turnover that's lower than the industry average may mean the company is carrying too much inventory, trying to sell the wrong stuff, or isn't doing as good a marketing job as its competitors.

> **|Best Tip**
>
> Low turnover often indicates that the company has too much of the wrong kind of goods.

Any combination of these situations would lower turnover and be bad news:

1. If the company's carrying too much inventory, it's tying up money unnecessarily (not to mention storage space and the people who keep records). Also, it has to pay interest on the funds it probably borrowed to pay suppliers.

2. An overstocked inventory means potential trouble if the company is selling seasonal or fashion merchandise that may be hard to unload later. (Just try selling snowmobiles in midsummer or marketing bell-bottom slacks or Nehru jackets to today's youth.)

3. Low turnover caused by the wrong selection of inventory means management may be out of touch with what the company's customers want to buy—stubbornly trying to sell them widgets when they really want gadgets, for example.

What if turnover's high? A turnover that's higher than the industry average may mean that the company's doing a better marketing job than its competitors, and that would be cause to throw a party. But before management starts sending out invitations, a high turnover could also mean that the business is stocking a lower average inventory than it should and not buying in large quantities. That could mean three things:

1. It's not getting the highest possible quantity discounts from suppliers.

2. It may be paying higher freight charges, because buying often and in small amounts usually forces you to ship by the most expensive methods.

3. It's paying too much. When prices are rising (as they usually are) buying often and in small quantities means you'll pay successively higher prices every time you buy.

So a higher-than-average turnover might be good or bad. Management won't know which until they check records, search their souls, call a few meetings, and reward or scare the hell out of whoever might be responsible, depending on the case.

Note: Although wholesalers and retailers must often carry a large inventory to accommodate the demands of their customers, manufacturers attempt to keep their inventories at a minimum. The practice of just-in-time inventory management in manufacturing has produced sizable savings in storage space, materials handling equipment, interest paid on borrowed funds, and other costs associated with carrying an inventory of materials and parts that go into an end product.

In the case of manufacturers, then, a zillion inventory turns could mean great things for a company.

Analyzing a Balance Sheet

Now let's revisit Figure 3-1 (it's on the next page) and pull off whatever numbers we need from there.

Current Ratio. Find this by dividing A.I.'s current assets by its current liabilities.

Avaricious Industries
Balance Sheet
December 31, 19XX

ASSETS

Current assets		
Cash and cash equivalents		$1,271,231
Accounts receivable	1,032,409	
less allowance for		
doubtful accounts	38,000	994,409
Notes receivable		350,000
Merchandise inventories		3,250,000
Total current assets		5,865,640
Property and equipment	17,841,980	
Less accumulated depreciation	4,173,130	
Net property and equipment		13,668,850
TOTAL ASSETS		$19,534,490

LIABILITIES

Current liabilities		
Accounts payable	1,275,300	
Salaries payable	330,000	
Income taxes payable	925,239	
Other accrued expenses	8,000	
Total current liabilities		2,538,539
Long-term liabilities		
Mortgage payable	500,000	
Bonds payable	2,400,000	
Total long-term liabilities		2,900,000
TOTAL LIABILITIES		5,438,539

STOCKHOLDERS' EQUITY

Common stock, 2,500,000 shares		
at $1 par value per share		2,500,000
Capital in excess of par value		1,750,000
Retained earnings, January 1,	8,386,350	
Net income for year	1,509,601	
Less dividends	(50,000)	
Retained earnings, December 31, 19xx		9,845,951
TOTAL STOCKHOLDERS' EQUITY		14,095,951
TOTAL LIABILITIES AND		
STOCKHOLDERS' EQUITY		$19,534,490

$$\frac{\text{Current assets}}{\text{Current liabilities}} = \frac{\$5,865,640}{\$2,538,539} = \$2.31 : \$1$$

The current ratio is a measure of safety. It tells you how many times the company could pay its current debts if it used its current assets to pay them with.

A.I.'s current ratio looks pretty solid. The company has $2.31 in current assets standing behind each $1 it owes in current debts. If this ratio were above, say, $3 : $1, it would imply that management had too many current assets (perhaps cash or inventory) that were just sitting there like a roomful of freeloading relatives instead of helping to make profits for the stockholders.

The acid-test ratio is a more realistic and practical measure of ability to pay current debts than the current ratio.

A current ratio may give you a false sense of security, though, because it includes some current assets (like inventory, for example) that can be hard to get rid of in a hurry if creditors are breaking down your doors. So a more realistic ratio that highlights a company's ability to pay its current bills is the next one.

Acid-test Ratio. The acid-test ratio is:

$$\frac{\text{Cash + Accounts receivable + Marketable securities}}{\text{Current liabilities}}$$

In A.I.'s case, that's

$$\frac{\$1,271,231 + \$994,409 + \$0}{\$2,538,539} = \frac{\$2,265,640}{\$2,538,539} = \$.89 : \$1$$

The acid-test ratio shows how well a company could pay its current debts using only its most liquid or "quick" assets. This is a more pessimistic—but also realistic—measure of safety than the current ratio, because it ignores sluggish, hard-to-liquidate current assets like inventory and notes receivable.

Instead, it adds up the three most liquid assets a business has:

cash (which is as liquid as you can get), accounts receivable (which will probably be collected in a month or so), and marketable securities (which could probably be sold with a telephone call).

A.I. seems to be fairly solid by this measure, too, with 89 cents in highly liquid assets standing behind each $1 it owes in current debts. If its acid-test ratio was, say, $1.50 : $1 and much of it was in cash, management might think about putting some of that cash to work by investing it in facilities or equipment, enhancing the company's marketing efforts, or doing something else to make more profit for stockholders.

If it were low, like $.5 : $1, management should worry. How's the company going to weather a quick, unforeseen storm?

Ratio of Debt to Stockholders' Equity. This calculation shows which group—creditors or stockholders—has the biggest stake in or the most control of the company. Observe:

$$\frac{\text{Total liabilities}}{\text{Stockholders' equity}} = \frac{\$\ 5{,}438{,}539}{\$14{,}095{,}951} = \$.39 : \$1$$

Creditors have 39 cents of claims against the company for each $1 of stockholders' claims.

A ratio of $1 to $1 would mean the company is worth as much to outsiders (creditors) as it is to its owners, which wouldn't be good news if you were a stockholder. In fact, it would mean that management is actually working half of every day for the company's creditors. What a miserable thought!

Best Tip

A healthy company has a ratio of debt to equity of 1 : 2 or better.

A high ratio here means that the company is heavily financed with debt (most likely bonds or long-term loans), which also means it's probably paying through the nose in interest each year—not to mention that the debt is going to come due some-day.

But good old A.I. is worth more than twice as much to stockholders than to creditors, which should make the stockholders happy. And happy stockholders mean that the top managers can probably feel safe trading in last year's Mercedes on a new model or adding a third vacation home.

Book Value of Common Stock. This is the theoretical amount per share that each stockholder would receive if the company's assets were sold on the balance sheet date. How much would that be if you were an A.I. stockholder?

$$\frac{\text{Stockholders' equity}}{\text{Common stock shares outstanding}} = \frac{\$14,095,951}{2,500,000} = \$5.64$$

So that's $5.64 per share. When the book value of a company's common stock is higher than its market value, investors usually consider the stock a good buy. A book value that's considerably less than market value, however, suggests that the stock may be overpriced on the market.

That doesn't necessarily mean that investors are being taken for a ride, however. Investors who are optimistic about a company's financial future may be perfectly willing to pay lots more for the stock on the open market than they'd get if the company were sold. But the greater the gap between book value and market value, the greater the risk.

Calculations That Use Data from Both Statements

Some calculations pull one figure off the income statement and one off the balance sheet. Calculators at the ready? Begin!

Rate of Return on Stockholders' Equity. This tells you how much profit management made on each dollar that stockholders invested in the company.

$$\frac{\text{Net income}}{\text{Stockholders' equity}} = \frac{\$ \ 1,509,601}{\$14,095,951} = .107 = 11 \text{ percent}$$

So A.I. made 11 cents (or 11 percent) this year on each of its stockholders' dollars. Again, it's important to have a comparative figure for companies in the same industry as A.I.

A high return suggests that management is doing a good job of managing the stockholders' investment. A low rate of return means that stockholders might consider investing their funds in some other company—or having the managers who are responsible for such lousy performance stoned publicly.

Best Tip

If the book value of a company's common stock is less than its market value, investors are paying more to own a share than they'd get if the company were liquidated.

If a company's return on equity is low, and the company is top-heavy with cash, management should put that excess cash to work to improve the return.

In A.I.'s case, stockholders who aren't satisfied with an 11 percent return should find someplace else to put their portions of the $14,095,951.

Keep in mind that return on equity changes every year as a company's net income changes.

Rate of Return on Total Assets. This calculation tells stockholders and creditors how well management is managing the company's assets. So we go shopping in the income statement and balance sheet to find:

$$\frac{\text{Net income}}{\text{Total assets}} \ = \ \frac{\$ \ 1,509,601}{\$19,534,490} \ = \ .077 = 8 \text{ percent}$$

A.I.'s management made about eight cents on each dollar's worth of assets this year. Is that good or bad? Once again, we don't know until we get a comparative figure for companies in the same industry. As with rate of return on stockholders' equity, a high figure suggests a good job; a low figure a not-so-good job.

Number Of Days Sales in Receivables. This is the corporate form of bondage, but not nearly as kinky. It shows how many days' worth of net sales are tied up in credit sales (accounts receivable) that haven't been collected yet. Sometimes this is called the average collection period. It can be figured in two steps.

Step 1: Figure average credit sales per day (let's assume that all A.I.'s sales are on credit):

$$\frac{\text{Net sales}}{365 \text{ days}} = \frac{\$38,028,500}{365} = \$104,188 \text{ average sales per day}$$

Step 2: Figure number of days sales tied up in receivables:

$$\frac{\$994,409 \text{ accounts receivable}}{\$104,188 \text{ average sales per day}} = 9.5 \text{ days}$$

The more days' worth of sales a company has tied up in accounts receivable, the worse things look. That's because the longer a debt goes uncollected, the greater the odds that it won't be collected. Any flinty-eyed corporate credit manager will tell you that.

Also, a lengthy collection period gives rise to that painful condition known as "paper profitability." Your income statement looks pretty good, but you don't actually have the money yet for the goods you've sold. More than a few "profitable" companies have gone down the tubes waiting for the money to come in. (Which is why watching cash flow is so important.)

A.I. is taking a mere 9.5 days to collect each credit sale. Because companies usually give credit customers 30 to 60 days maximum to pay their bills (except for some industries like the grocery business, where 5 to 7 days is the norm), A.I. is collecting from credit customers very fast, which is very good.

Best Tip
A company with a long average collection period is probably selling to marginal credit customers and/or not working hard enough to collect past-due balances.

That implies that the company's credit manager isn't approving open-book accounts to many slow pay/no-pay/day-late-and-

Best Tip

A long collection period may mean you're profitable on paper—while you're sinking fast.

a-dollar-short customers. He may, in fact, be running them off at gunpoint for even having the guts to ask. Moreover, the company is probably offering cash discounts for early payment, which motivates customers to pay up pronto.

If the number of days sales tied up in receivables were, say, 35 or 40, management should probably:

- Be much more choosy about the companies A.I. sells to on account.
- Consider offering cash discounts to encourage customers to pay their bills earlier than necessary.
- Pursue deadbeat accounts more aggressively to collect past-due balances.
- Encourage the credit manager to update his or her résumé and start applying for work with competitors.

As with many other financial-analysis calculations, a comparative figure for the industry will put this calculation in a better perspective.

Try a Little Vertical Analysis

Vertical analysis shows how a company's condition changed from one year to the next. It compares the statements top to bottom for the past two years by expressing their key amounts as percentages of a base figure (100 percent).

When you analyze an income statement vertically, net sales is usually used as the base. On a balance sheet, total assets are the base for the assets side and the sum of liabilities and stockholders' equity is the base for those elements.

Vertical analysis can show you:

- If cost of goods sold increased or decreased since last year.
- Whether gross profit increased or decreased from last year. (Note: If cost of goods sold increased, gross profit auto-

matically decreased. If cost of goods sold decreased, gross profit automatically increased.)

- Whether the company made more or less profit as a percentage of net sales from last year to this year.
- Which factors (cost of goods sold, expenses, or both) combined to make the company's net income a higher or lower percentage of net sales than it was last year.
- Whether selling and general-and-administrative expenses increased or decreased as a percentage of net sales.
- How much income tax the company pays as a percentage of net sales.
- The percentage change in the company's current and property and equipment assets (as a percentage of total assets) from last year to this year.
- The percentage change in the company's current and long-term liabilities (as a percentage of liabilities and stockholders' equity) from last year to this year.
- The percentage change in each stockholders' equity item (as a percentage of liabilities and stockholders' equity) from last year to this year.

The Income Statement. Figure 5-1 on the next page shows a vertical analysis for A.I.'s income statement for this year and last year, using net sales as a base (100 percent). All those interested folks you read about in chapter one can compare the change in percentages between years to see what's gone up or down, by how much, and which items accounted for the difference, and whether it's good (yea!) or bad (boo!).

Notice that net income as a percentage of net sales is 1.3 percent lower this year than last. That was caused by a combination of three factors. Cost of goods sold increased 6.5 percent, which is *not* good news. That automatically lowered gross profit by the same percentage.

Total expenses were down this year by 4.3 percent, and income tax was down by .9 percent, but that wasn't enough to offset that 6.5 percent increase in cost of goods sold. So net

Figure 5-1   **Avaricious Industries**
Consolidated Earnings Statement
(Note: Comparative statements are condensed to key amounts)

	This Year		Last Year	
	Amount	Percent	Amount	Percent
Net sales	$38,028,500	100.0%	$26,315,420	100.00%
Cost of goods sold	26,358,500	69.3%	16,526,084	62.80%
Gross profit	11,670,000	30.7%	9,789,336	37.20%
Variable and selling expenses	6,910,605	18.2%	6,157,808	23.40%
General and administrative expenses	2,324,555	6.1%	1,368,402	5.20%
Total operating expenses	9,235,160	24.3%	7,526,210	28.60%
Earnings before income tax	2,434,840	6.4%	2,263,126	8.60%
Income tax	925,239	2.4%	868,409	3.30%
Net income	$1,509,601	4.0%	$1,394,717	5.30%
Common stock shares outstanding	2,500,000		2,498,750	
Earnings per share of common stock	0.60		0.56	

income, expressed as a percentage of net sales, decreased 1.3 percent, and the higher cost of goods sold was the root cause.

The Balance Sheet. Shifting to A.I.'s balance sheet, Figure 5-2 expresses key assets as a percentage of total assets for the past two years. Some changes are obvious. As with the income statement, liabilities and stockholders' equity are expressed as a percentage of their total (percentage amounts may vary because of rounding).

First, take a look at the company's assets. Notice that cash is a higher percentage of assets this year than last year (6.51 percent vs. 3.82 percent). Accounts receivable are also a higher percentage of assets, but notes receivable dropped slightly. Merchandise inventory was lower than last year (which implies more careful

Figure 5-2	**Avaricious Industries** **Balance Sheet** **December 31, 19XX**			
ASSETS	*This Year*		*Last Year*	
Current assets	Amount	Percent	Amount	Percent
Cash and cash				
equivalents	$1,271,231	6.51%	$677,600	3.82%
Accounts				
receivable (net)	994,409	5.09%	773,134	4.35%
Notes receivable	350,000	1.79%	320,000	1.80%
Merchandise				
inventories	3,250,000	16.64%	4,190,000	23.59%
Total				
current assets	5,865,640	30.03%	5,960,734	33.56%
Property and				
equipment (net)	13,668,850	69.97%	11,798,155	66.44%
TOTAL ASSETS	$19,534,490	100%	$17,758,889	100%

inventory management) and net property and equipment increased, because management bought some new items and unloaded some obsolete ones (which was shown on the cash flow statement).

Moving to liabilities (next page), you'll see that accounts payable is a smaller percentage of total liabilities and stockholders' equity this year than last. Income taxes payable are somewhat higher, but other accrued expenses ("accrued," recall, means owed but not yet paid on the balance sheet date) are considerably lower. Looking at the two major liability categories, current liabilities are up .21 percent over last year, but long-term liabilities are 1.34 percent below last year's percentage. The net result? Total liabilities are 1.15 percent lower this year. So creditors have less of a stake in the company this year than they had last year. Cheers!

Stockholders' equity is up 1.15 percent, which is logical, because debts went down 1.15 percent. The decrease in the creditors' claims naturally shifted down to (and increased) the stockholders' claims.

Figure 5-2, continued

LIABILITIES

	This Year		Last Year	
	Amount	Percent	Amount	Percent
Current liabilities				
Accounts payable	1,275,300	6.53%	1,477,800	8.32%
Salaries payable	330,000	1.69%	245,200	1.38%
Income taxes payable	925,239	4.74%	500,200	2.82%
Other accrued expenses	8,000	0.04%	48,339	0.27%
Total current liabilities	2,538,539	13.00%	2,271,539	12.79%
Long-term liabilities				
Mortgage payable	500,000	2.56%	536,000	3.02%
Bonds payable	2,400,000	12.29%	2,340,000	13.18%
Total long-term liabilities	2,900,000	14.85%	2,876,000	16.19%
TOTAL LIABILITIES	5,438,539	27.84%	5,147,539	28.99%

STOCKHOLDERS' EQUITY

	This Year		Last Year	
Common stock, 2,500,000 shares at $1 par value per share	2,500,000	12.80%	2,498,750	14.07%
Capital in excess of par value	1,750,000	8.96%	1,726,250	9.72%
Retained earnings, January 1, 19XX	8,386,350	42.93%	6,991,633	39.37%
Net income for year	1,509,601	7.73%	1,424,717	8.02%
Less dividends	(50,000)	-0.26%	(30,000)	-0.17%
Retained earnings, Dec. 31, 19XX	9,845,951	50.40%	8,386,350	47.22%
TOTAL STOCKHOLDERS' EQUITY	14,095,951	72.16%	12,611,350	71.01%
TOTAL LIABILITIES AND STOCKHOLDERS' EQUITY	$19,534,490	100.00%	$17,758,889	100.00%

The Agile Manager's Checklist

✔ Look at the organization's finances from several angles. Some indicators may show it's doing fine, while others may show it's doing poorly.

✔ Find an industry comparison for all your figures. When in doubt, try the *Robert Morris Annual Statement Studies*. (You'll find it in most good libraries.)

✔ A healthy current ratio is $2 : $1 (current assets vs. current liabilities).

✔ The acid-test ratio (cash and accounts receivable vs. current liabilities) should be around $1 : $1.

✔ Return on stockholders' equity (net income divided by stockholders' equity) should at least match the return investors could get elsewhere.

✔ Many companies live or die based on how fast they turn over inventory.

Chapter Six

Inventory Valuation (Or, What's It Worth?)

"*Bankrupt companies value their inventory with a method called FISH. That stands for First In, Still Here.*"

ANONYMOUS

As the Agile Manager jotted down a few notes about valuing inventory for his meeting with Steve, he recalled meeting with a small vendor when that very subject came up.

He'd just about wrapped up the visit with the company's president when the president took a phone call. The Agile Manager cursed himself for not getting out of there a hair sooner—especially when the president began shouting at his caller.

"LIFO Schmifo! I just want you to get that bottom line down!" The man's bald head turned purple.

Wow, thought the Agile Manager. Do people like this still exist in this industry?

"Don't give me that crap—I pay you to keep my books, not tell me what to do. Now go back at it and don't call me until you have the bottom line in six figures." With that he slammed down the *phone, mopped his brow, and became remarkably composed in just a few seconds.*

"Damn accountant," he said to the Agile Manager. "Tells me I can't change inventory valuation methods every year to suit my needs. But I tell you," he hissed through gritted teeth, "I can't afford to give the government half my profits!" His head purpled again briefly. "Well," he said, smiling broadly and sticking out his hand. "Pleasure meeting you finally. Next time let's do it over lunch."

Companies have a number of methods at hand to figure out the value of their year-end inventory, and each one produces a different value for the same goods.

The ending inventory's value, as you saw in chapters two and three (we've come a long way, baby!), shows up on both the income statement and the balance sheet. The method a company picks to assign a value to that inventory will alter the value of its assets (because inventory is an asset) as well as the cost of goods sold—which also affects, in domino fashion, gross profit and net income, and ultimately stockholders' equity.

Major Inventory Valuation Methods

The philosophical question, "What's in a name?" might be changed to read, "What's an inventory worth?" Fiscal philosophers and monetary mavens can answer that question four different ways.

Specific invoice prices. This valuation method is pretty unusual. It only works when a company's records allow it to track each item in its ending inventory to the specific invoice on which the item was bought.

Specific invoice prices would be practical for auto dealerships or businesses that sell heavy equipment, because their ending inventory would be made up of big-ticket, easily identified products. All you need to do is walk out on the lot and check the serial numbers on the cars or bulldozers, look them up in the invoices in the file, and jot down each one's cost.

FIFO. No, we're not talking about somebody's pet poodle.

FIFO stands for First In, First Out, and it refers to how the units in the company's inventory flowed through the warehouse from when they arrived until the time they were sold. Most products move through a business in FIFO fashion. The first ones received are the first ones sold over the counter to customers.

Now if you assume this sequence reflects reality, it stands to reason that the ending inventory (the goods that are sitting in the warehouse on the last day of the year) are the ones that were bought most recently. Very good! The cost of the goods that were sold, then, would be the total of the beginning inventory and the earliest purchases.

Look at Figure 6-1, which shows information about Avaricious Industries' beginning inventory and the purchases it made

Figure 6-1	*Units*	*Cost per unit*	*Total cost*
Beginning inventory	274,754	$15.25	$4,190,000
February purchase	313,036	$12.18	$3,812,775
April purchase	559,386	$11.36	$6,354,625
June purchase	421,884	$12.05	$5,083,700
September purchase	762,555	$10.00	$7,625,550
November purchase	203,348	$12.50	$2,541,850
TOTAL UNITS	2,534,963		
TOTAL PURCHASES			$25,418,500
Goods available for sale			$29,608,500
Weighted average cost per unit		$11.68	

If ending inventory is 274,163 units:

Value under FIFO:	203,348 @ $12.50	2,541,850
	70,815 @ $10.00	708,150
		$3,250,000
Value under LIFO:	274,163 @ 15.25	4,180,986
		$4,180,986

Value under WEIGHTED AVERAGE:

	274,163 @ $11.68	$3,202,224

during the year. Using FIFO, the ending inventory is assumed to consist of the most recent purchases (which is all of November's purchase plus a few left over from September's buy—a total of 274,163 units). Their value comes to $3,250,000. Okay so far?

The cost of goods sold and net income would then be $26,358,500 and $1,509,601 respectively. See Figure 6-2 for how all that shakes out on A.I.'s income statement.

As you can see, this income statement is identical to the one you met back in chapter two. That's because A.I. uses FIFO to value its inventory.

LIFO. LIFO assumes that the *last* units received were the first ones sold (Last In, First Out). That doesn't jibe with the way most inventory usually flows through a business, except for things that might be stored in bins like nuts and bolts.

But we can assume a theoretical LIFO movement nevertheless. If we do, then the ending inventory (the goods sitting in the warehouse on December 31) are leftovers from last January's beginning inventory.

Why would any company choose to value inventory in a way that contradicts the real flow of goods through a company? We'll get to that in a few pages.

Look at Figure 6-1 again. Using LIFO, the units in A.I.'s ending inventory—274,163 pieces—are presumed to be leftovers from the 274,754 pieces it started the year with, so they would be valued at $4,180,986 (which, you'll notice, is $930,986 more than the ending inventory's FIFO value).

That changes all the numbers—for the better. The cost of goods sold and net income would then be $25,427,514 and $2,086,812 respectively.

Figure 6-3 shows how A.I.'s income statement would look if ending inventory and cost of goods sold were valued by the

---

Best Tip

Most businesses will find it difficult if not impossible to use the specific invoice method to value inventory.

Figure 6-2: Income statement under FIFO

Avaricious Industries
Consolidated Earnings Statement
For Year Ended December 31, 19XX

Net sales		$38,028,500
Cost of goods sold:		
Inventory, January 1	4,190,000	
Purchases (net)	25,418,500	
Goods available for sale	29,608,500	
Less inventory, December 31	3,250,000	
Cost of goods sold:		26,358,500
Gross profit		11,670,000
Operating expenses		
Selling:		
Sales salaries expense	1,991,360	
Advertising expense	3,527,650	
Sales promotion expense	987,745	
Depreciation expense—		
selling equipment	403,850	6,910,605
General and administrative:		
Office salaries expense	1,124,650	
Repairs expense	112,655	
Utilities expense	39,700	
Insurance expense	48,780	
Equipment expense	63,750	
Interest expense	211,020	
Misc. expenses	650,100	
Depreciation expense—		
office equipment	73,900	2,324,555
Total operating expenses		9,235,160
Earnings before income tax		2,434,840
Income tax		925,239
Net income		$1,509,601
Common stock shares outstanding:		2,500,000
Earnings per share of common stock:		$0.60

Figure 6-3: Income statement under LIFO

Avaricious Industries
Consolidated Earnings Statement
For Year Ended December 31, 19XX

Net sales		$38,028,500
Cost of goods sold:		
Inventory, January 1	4,190,000	
Purchases (net)	25,418,500	
Goods available for sale	29,608,500	
Less inventory, December 31	4,180,986	
Cost of goods sold:		25,427,514
Gross profit		12,600,986
Operating expenses		
Selling:		
Sales salaries expense	1,991,360	
Advertising expense	3,527,650	
Sales promotion expense	987,745	
Depreciation expense—		
selling equipment	403,850	6,910,605
General and administrative:		
Office salaries expense	1,124,650	
Repairs expense	112,655	
Utilities expense	39,700	
Insurance expense	48,780	
Equipment expense	63,750	
Interest expense	211,020	
Misc. expenses	650,100	
Depreciation expense—		
office equipment	73,900	2,324,555
Total operating expenses		9,235,160
Earnings before income tax		3,365,826
Income tax		1,279,014
Net income		$2,086,812
Common stock shares outstanding:		2,500,000
Earnings per share of common stock:		$0.83

company accountants under a LIFO assumption.

Because the value of the inventory using LIFO is $930,986 higher than FIFO, that automatically makes the cost of goods sold $930,986 *lower* and net income $930,986 higher. Think this through a couple of times (we'll wait). It makes sense. If the ending inventory is higher, cost of goods sold is less. If cost of goods sold is less, then net income grows. And in this case, the difference between FIFO and LIFO made darn nearly $1 million difference in the company's profit picture (pre-tax). But we're not done yet.

Weighted Average. Here's yet another way to assign a value to an ending inventory. Go back to loyal old Figure 6-1 again (it must be getting tired by now), and you'll see a weighted average cost per unit of $11.68. Where did that come from? Well, A.I. had a total of 2,534,963 units available for sale this year (the sum of its be-

How you value inventory can make a big difference in the net income for a given year.

ginning inventory plus all its purchases), and the total cost was $29,608,500. The weighted average cost per unit?

$$\frac{\$29,608,500}{2,534,963 \text{ units}} = \$11.68$$

$11.68 X 274,163 units in ending inventory = $3,202,224

Figure 6-4 on the following page shows how Avaricious Industries' income statement would look in that situation. Naturally, the cost of goods sold and net income are different from the amounts you saw on either the FIFO or LIFO income statements.

If you value A.I.'s ending inventory using the weighted average method, the net income ends up being $29,621 less than it was under FIFO and $606,832 less than it was under LIFO. Quite a difference, but that's the way it is.

Figure 6-4: Income statement under weighted average

Avaricious Industries
Consolidated Earnings Statement
For Year Ended December 31, 19XX

Net sales			$38,028,500
Cost of goods sold:			
Inventory, January 1		4,190,000	
Purchases (net)		25,418,500	
Goods available for sale		29,608,500	
Less inventory, December 31		3,202,224	
Cost of goods sold:			26,406,276
Gross profit			11,622,224
Operating expenses			
Selling:			
Sales salaries expense	1,991,360		
Advertising expense	3,527,650		
Sales promotion expense	987,745		
Depreciation expense—			
selling equipment	403,850	6,910,605	
General and administrative:			
Office salaries expense	1,124,650		
Repairs expense	112,655		
Utilities expense	39,700		
Insurance expense	48,780		
Equipment expense	63,750		
Interest expense	211,020		
Misc. expenses	650,100		
Depreciation expense—			
office equipment	73,900	2,324,555	
Total operating expenses			9,235,160
Earnings before income tax			2,387,064
Income tax			907,084
Net income			$1,479,980
Common stock shares outstanding:			2,500,000
Earnings per share of common stock:			$0.59

The company's balance sheet, of course, would reflect a corresponding change in the value of its assets (because inventory is an asset) and stockholders' equity (because net income on the income statement is added to the beginning retained earnings balance to produce the year-end retained earnings balance).

Be Consistent

Companies will typically pick one method for valuing their ending inventory and cost of goods sold and stick with it for several years. If they don't, their accounting statements won't be comparable from one year to the next. That makes it difficult to do the year-to-year vertical analysis comparisons you learned about in the last chapter.

There's no "best" way to value inventory, but you must be consistent from year to year.

Also, companies can't just opt for the method that makes the bottom line look the best each year. The IRS won't allow it.

The inventory valuation method that a company uses should be mentioned either on the financial statement itself or in the notes at the end of the statements.

Which One's Best?

There is no "best" way to value inventory, and all are legal. When prices are rising, FIFO will assign the highest cost to inventory and the lowest to cost of goods sold, thus producing the highest net income. LIFO would do the opposite, assigning the lowest cost to inventory and the highest to cost of goods sold, resulting in a lower net income than FIFO. In times of rising prices, weighted average would produce amounts somewhere between those of FIFO and LIFO.

During times of high inflation, such as the late 1970s and early 1980s, many companies changed to LIFO to get a tax break, because it yielded the lowest taxable income. It's important to realize, however, that the Internal Revenue Service requires companies that want to use LIFO for tax-reporting purposes use it for financial reporting purposes too. In such cases, notes at the end of the financial statements may show the value of the inven tory and cost of goods sold under other methods such as FIFO or weighted average.

LIFO and FIFO are the most popular of the four valuation methods. Companies sometimes prefer to use LIFO for financial reporting purposes. That's because it not only produces the lowest taxable income in times of rising prices, but also because it assigns the most recent prices to cost of goods sold.

The Agile Manager's Checklist

✔ The method a company uses to value its ending inventory will affect its assets, cost of goods sold, gross profit, net income, and retained earnings.

✔ An inventory may be valued using four methods: specific invoice prices, FIFO, LIFO, and weighted average.

✔ Companies must use the same inventory valuation method each year if they want the information on their financial statements to be comparable from one year to the next. Also, the IRS requires it.

Chapter Seven

Depreciation

"It's better to wear out than rust out."

ANONYMOUS

"Depreciation is one of those things, Steve, that shows why cash flow is so important," said the Agile Manager.

This was the final training session for Steve. Good thing, too, thought the Agile Manager before the meeting. I've been neglecting some important things. But this'll pay off in the long run. Steve can start doing ratios for me—and I'll get him working on cost estimates and figuring price points.

"The money you spent on the car or computer or whatever is long gone," he continued, "but you might take deductions for five, seven, or ten years. That's why your profits may be down while cash is actually up."

Steve seemed to drink it in. "Hmm. But if you took the big hit all at once—like you deducted $800,000 for a machine in one year—then your profits would sink to the floor of the Grand Canyon."

"Darn tootin'. But the idea is that the machine goes on making

77

you money for many years, so you should deduct a little bit as long as it's in use."

"I get it," Steve said. "You know, this isn't so bad. I don't know what I was afraid of."

"All you were afraid of, dear boy, was the unknown."

The philosophy embodied in the quote leading off this chapter applies just as well to a company's machinery and equipment as it does to your body. Companies, however, can deduct the annual wear-out (or depreciation) on equipment, buildings, and other expensive assets as a business expense each year. That decreases their taxable income. (Unfortunately, the IRS refuses to let us taxpayers do that with our bodies, darn it. How about some *real* tax reform?)

Depreciation is how a company recovers the high cost of its costly assets gradually, over the course of the years they'll be used in the business.

Best Tip

Depreciation is an estimate. Technology, routine maintenance, and other factors affect how long a machine will actually run before it has to be replaced.

This makes sense. To record the entire $2 million cost of a new machine as an expense in the year it was bought would really clobber net income that year, plus it wouldn't be fair. That one particular year would take a nuclear hit in expenses for a machine that might actually run for ten or fifteen years.

Each year's depreciation throughout the machine's life is matched, therefore, against the net sales that the machine helped the company make that year. (That's called "the matching principle of accounting," by the way.)

Types of Depreciation

Depreciation can be either physical or technological. Both types reduce an asset's value.

Physical depreciation is simply wear and tear. Example? Check out how rough a company's delivery trucks look after they've been driven on salted roads up north for several winters.

Technological depreciation happens to everything from mainframe computers to photocopying machines and laser surgery equipment, because high-

Best Tip

Depreciation can be physical, technological, or both.

tech will eventually be replaced by higher-tech. When that happens, the equipment ends up being sold or used for a doorstop or a planter.

Some Preliminary Details

Before we go charging off in all directions, let's look at a few ideas about an asset's true cost for depreciation purposes.

Depreciation starts with the asset's cost, but "cost" includes both actual cost *plus* everything the company paid to get the machine delivered, installed, shined, sheened, polished and glossed, and up and running. That would include, for example, freight charges, unpacking, changes to existing facilities (such as pouring a concrete-reinforced base or installing customized wiring), and other relevant items.

Keep in mind, too, that depreciation is an estimate. Equipment that's well maintained may last many years past its estimated life, while machines that are run half to death—and only noticed when they break down—die before their time.

Responsible managers naturally treat the company's equipment as they would their best friends (witness the recently celebrated "Take a Drill Press to Lunch" week), because equipment tends to treat you as well as you treat it. The '78 Ford LTD II that I bought new has got more than 194,000 miles on it with nary a major breakdown or wreck. Everything works. (No, it's not for sale.)

You can calculate depreciation using one of a few methods.

Most of these acknowledge an asset's *salvage value*, which is how much management figures it'll be worth at the end of its useful life. That value might be how much management thinks it would get on a trade-in or if the machine were sold for scrap.

As an example, let's set up a hypothetical machine. We'll call it a nit-picker; no doubt you've run into several of them in the accounting department. Here's the lowdown:

- Our model, the 386-PA (Partially Awesome), came with a 800 MHz Pentium chip, built-in compass, neat secret compartment, and fat-gram counter. It cost $16,000, including all that installation stuff that was mentioned above.

- Management estimates that the 386-PA will run faithfully for five years and be worth $2,000 when it's finally put out to pasture. That means it'll be depreciated a total of $14,000 ($16,000-$2,000).

- The 386-PA is a piece of production equipment (batteries not included) that the manufacturer claims will pick 80,000 nits during its lifetime.

Let's crank up our calculators and depreciate this beast four different ways.

> | **Best Tip**
>
> Straight-line depreciation is the easiest to figure and is often used for reporting to stockholders.

Straight-Line Depreciation

This method depreciates an asset the same amount each year for its estimated life. The formula is:

$$\frac{\text{Cost–Salvage value}}{\text{Estimated years of service}} = \frac{\$14,000}{5} = \$2,800 \text{ per year}$$

On its income statement, A.I. would record a depreciation expense of $2,800 on the nit-picker each year. Then it would add that to the running total in an account called "accumulated depreciation." The total in that account is subtracted from the machine's original cost on the balance sheet (see page 30) to come up with its book value on the balance sheet date.

At the end of its five-year life, the machine would be fully depreciated. The company wouldn't record any more depreciation af-

ter five years even if the nit-picker is still going like the Energizer Rabbit. The company's books for this machine (in case you're interested) would look like this under straight-line:

Year	Depreciation Expense	Accumulated Depreciation	Book Value
1	$2,800	$2,800	$13,200
2	$2,800	$5,600	$10,400
3	$2,800	$8,400	$7,600
4	$2,800	$11,200	$4,800
5	$2,800	$14,000	$2,000

Units of Production

The units of production technique relates a machine's depreciation to the number of units it makes each accounting period. The only catch is, the operator (or somebody—probably a computer) has to keep track of the machine's output each year. What fun.

The formula for depreciation per unit under this approach is:

$$\frac{\text{Cost–Salvage value}}{\text{Estimated units of production (over its life)}} =$$

$$\frac{\$14,000}{80,000} = \$.175 \text{ depreciation per unit}$$

If the machine made the following number of nits each year, its depreciation would be:

Year	Nits Produced	Depreciation Per Nit	Yearly Depreciation
1	11,250	X .175	$ 1,968.75
2	15,580	X .175	$ 2,726.50
3	18,390	X 175	$ 3,218.25
4	19,470	X .175	$ 3,407.25
5	15,100	X .175	$ 2,642.50
	79,790		$13,963.25

Note: The company could depreciate the machine $36.75 in its sixth year (210 nits' worth), because it only made 79,790 during its first five years and this method depreciates by units, not by years. But then, this is *really* nit-picking.

Declining Balance

The declining balance method figures depreciation each accounting period by applying a fixed rate to the asset's book value. That's its value when you subtract accumulated depreciation from its cost.

Best Tip

Both declining balance and sum-of-the-years' digits are accelerated methods that depreciate equipment heavily in its newer years.

The declining balance method doesn't take the asset's salvage value off the front end, as the other two did. Instead, it stops when the asset's book value hits its salvage value.

The "fixed rate" mentioned above is usually twice the straight-line rate, which is why this method is often called the "double declining balance method." It's an accelerated method that increases depreciation in a machine's newer years and decreases it as it gets older.

In this case, the machine has five years of expected life. That means the depreciation rate would be (1/5 X 2) or 40 percent each year on the nit-picker's value. Each year's depreciation would be:

Year 1   ($16,000 - $0) X .40 = $6,400
Year 2   ($16,000-$6,400) X .40 = $3,840
Year 3   ($16,000-$6,400-$3,840) X .40 = $2,304
Year 4   ($16,000-$6,400-$3,840-$2,304) X .40 = $1,382 $13,926
Year 5 ($16,000-$6,400-$3,840-$2,304-$1,382) X .40 = $ ~~829~~   <u>74</u>
                                                        <u>$14,000</u>

See how the depreciation in year five was cut back? Since this is the declining balance method, accumulated depreciation must stop at $14,000. Anything more would cut into the machine's $2,000 salvage value. That's why the machine can be depreciated only $74 in year five.

Sum-of-the-Years' Digits

This technique, like declining balance, is also an accelerated method. It makes the sum of the digits in the machine's expected life the denominator for a series of yearly depreciation fractions. The numerators of these fractions are the machine's years of life *in reverse order*, which means a steadily smaller depreciation fraction is applied to the asset's value (cost-salvage value) each year.

The sum-of-the-years' digits for the nit picker is 1+2+3+4+5 = 15. Here we go!

Year 1	5/15 X $14,000	=	$4,667
Year 2	4/15 X $14,000	=	$3,733
Year 3	3/15 X $14,000	=	$2,800
Year 4	2/15 X $14,000	=	$1,867
Year 5	1/15 X $14,000	=	<u>$933</u>
			<u>$14,000</u>

A Word About MACRS

MACRS stands for Modified Accelerated Cost Recovery System (sure, you knew that!). It was set up by the IRS under the Tax Reform Act of 1986 as a depreciation method for federal income tax purposes. All fixed assets installed after December 31, 1986, have to use the MACRS method, which is a lot like the sum-of-the-years' digits and declining balance methods.

Under MACRS, there are eight categories of assets distinguished by their estimated useful lives. The categories range from 3-year property (such as over-the-road tractors) to 31.5-year property (office buildings). The IRS, helpful souls that they are, provides tables with depreciation rates to be applied each year of an asset's life.

Although it's not unusual for companies to use MACRS for both tax and financial reporting purposes, many firms use the straight-line method for financial reporting (like the kind that appears in an annual report). That's because of its consistent impact on net income from one year to the next.

The Agile Manager's Checklist

✔ You recover the cost of a high-priced piece of equipment gradually by depreciating it.

✔ Depreciation can be figured using four methods:

■ *Straight line* racks up an equal amount of depreciation expense against an asset each year of its useful life.

■ *Units of production* depreciates a machine according to what it made each year.

■ *Declining balance* and *sum-of-the-years'-digits* both charge more depreciation expense against a machine in its newer years.

✔ You don't depreciate equipment past its estimated salvage or scrap value.

Glossary

ACCOUNTS PAYABLE. Amounts a company owes to creditors.

ACCOUNTS RECEIVABLE. Amounts owed to a company by customers that it sold to on credit. Total accounts receivable are usually reduced by an allowance for doubtful accounts.

ACID-TEST RATIO. A ratio that shows how well a company could pay its current debts using only its most liquid or "quick" assets. It's a more pessimistic—but also realistic—measure of safety than the current ratio, because it ignores sluggish, hard-to-liquidate current assets like inventory and notes receivable. Here's the formula:

$$\frac{\text{Cash} + \text{Accounts receivable} + \text{Marketable securities}}{\text{Current liabilities}}$$

ACCRUAL. A method of accounting in which you record expenses when you incur them and sales as you make them—not when you pay bills or receive checks in the mail.

ASSETS. Anything of value that a company owns.

BALANCE SHEET. A "snapshot" statement that freezes a company on a particular day, like the last day of the year, and shows

85

the balances in its asset, liability, and stockholders' equity accounts. It's governed by the formula Assets = Liabilities + Stockholders' Equity.

BOND. A long-term, interest-bearing promissory note that companies may use to borrow money for periods of time such as five, ten, or twenty years.

BOOK VALUE. An asset's cost basis minus accumulated depreciation.

BOOK VALUE OF COMMON STOCK. The theoretical amount per share that each stockholder would receive if a company's assets were sold on the balance sheet's date. Book value equals:

$$\frac{\text{Stockholders' equity}}{\text{Common stock shares outstanding}}$$

CAPITAL. The money, raised by selling stock or bonds or taking out loans, that you use to start, operate, and grow a business.

CAPITAL IN EXCESS OF PAR VALUE. What a company collected when it sold stock for more than the par value per share.

CASH AND CASH EQUIVALENTS. The balance in a company's checking account(s) plus short-term or temporary investments (sometimes called "marketable securities"), which are highly liquid.

CASH-FLOW STATEMENT. A statement that shows where a company's cash came from and where it went for a period of time, such as a year.

CASH FLOWS FROM FINANCING ACTIVITIES. A section on the cash-flow statement that shows how much cash a company raised by selling stocks or bonds this year and how much was paid out for cash dividends and other finance-related obligations.

CASH FLOWS FROM INVESTING ACTIVITIES. A section on the cash-flow statement that shows how much cash came in and went out because of various investing activities like purchasing machinery.

CASH FLOWS FROM OPERATIONS. A section on the cash-flow

statement that shows how much cash came into a company and how much went out during the normal course of business.

Cost basis. An asset's purchase price, plus costs associated with the purchase, like installation fees, taxes, etc.

Cost of goods sold. The cost of merchandise that a company sold this year. For manufacturing companies, the cost of raw materials, components, labor and other things that went into producing an item.

Current assets. Cash, things that will be converted into cash within a year (such as accounts receivable), and inventory.

Current liabilities. Bills a company must pay within the next twelve months.

Current ratio. A ratio that shows how many times a company could pay its current debts if it used its current assets to pay them. The formula:

$$\frac{\text{Current assets}}{\text{Current liabilities}}$$

Declining balance. An accelerated depreciation method that calculates depreciation each year by applying a fixed rate to the asset's book (cost–accumulated depreciation) value. Depreciation stops when the asset's book value reaches its salvage value.

Depreciation. A technique by which a company recovers the high cost of its plant-and-equipment assets gradually during the number of years they'll be used in the business. Depreciation can be physical, technological, or both.

Dividend. A payment a company makes to stockholders.

Earnings before income tax. The profit a company made before income taxes.

Earnings per share of common stock. How much profit a company made on each share of common stock this year.

FIFO (First In, First Out). An inventory valuation method that presumes that the first units received were the first ones sold.

GENERAL-AND-ADMINISTRATIVE EXPENSES. What was spent to run the non-sales and non-manufacturing part of a company, such as office salaries and interest paid on loans.

GROSS PROFIT. The profit a company makes before expenses and taxes are taken away.

INCOME STATEMENT. An accounting statement that summarizes information about a company in the following format:

> Net Sales
> − Cost of goods sold
> Gross profit
> − Operating expenses
> Earnings before income tax
> − Income tax
> = Net income or (Net loss)

Formally called a "consolidated earnings statement," it covers a period of time such as a quarter or a year.

INCOME TAX. What the business paid to the IRS.

INVENTORY TURNOVER. The number of times a company sold out and replaced its average stock of goods in a year. The formula is:

$$\frac{\text{Cost of goods sold}}{\text{Average inventory (beginning inventory + ending)/2}}$$

LIABILITIES. What a company owes to its creditors. In other words, debts.

LIFO (Last In, First Out). An inventory valuation method that presumes that the last units received were the first ones sold.

LONG-TERM LIABILITIES. Bills that are payable in more than one year, such as a mortgage or bonds.

MACRS (Modified Accelerated Cost Recovery System). A depreciation method created by the IRS under the Tax Reform Act of 1986. Companies must use it to depreciate all plant and equipment assets installed after December 31, 1986 (for tax purposes).

MERCHANDISE INVENTORY. The value of the products that a

retailing or wholesaling company intends to resell for a profit. In a manufacturing business, inventories would include finished goods, goods in process, raw materials, and parts and components that will go into the end product.

NET INCOME. The profit a company makes after cost of goods sold, expenses, and taxes are subtracted from net sales.

NET SALES (revenue). The amount sold after customers' returns, sales discounts, and other allowances are taken away from gross sales. (Companies usually just show the net sales amount on their income statements, omitting returns, allowances, and the like.)

NOTES RECEIVABLE. Notes receivable are promissory notes that the company has accepted from its debtors. Most promissory notes pay interest. Those that are due within a year are shown under "Current Assets." Those that mature in more than a year would be listed under "Long-term Assets." If a note is being collected in installments, the payments due within the next twelve months are shown as a current asset, and the remainder is shown as a long-term asset.

NUMBER OF DAYS SALES IN RECEIVABLES (average collection period). The number of days of net sales that are tied up in credit sales (accounts receivable) that haven't been collected yet.

OPERATING EXPENSES. The total amount that was spent to run a company this year.

PAR VALUE. An arbitrary value that a company may assign to its stock. Par value has no relationship to what the stock is selling for on the open market.

PROFIT. What's left over after you subtract the cost of goods sold and all your expenses from sales.

PROPERTY AND EQUIPMENT. Assets such as land, buildings, machinery, and equipment that the business will use for several years to make the product or provide the service that it sells. They are shown at the cost a company paid to buy or build them minus the amount they've depreciated since they were bought or built. (Except for land, which is not depreciated.)

RATE OF RETURN ON STOCKHOLDERS' EQUITY. The percentage return or profit that management made on each dollar stockholders invested in a company. Here's how you figure it:

$$\frac{\text{Net income}}{\text{Stockholders' equity}}$$

RATE OF RETURN ON TOTAL ASSETS. The percentage return or profit that management made on each dollar of assets. The formula is:

$$\frac{\text{Net income}}{\text{Total assets}}$$

RATIO OF DEBT TO STOCKHOLDERS' EQUITY. A ratio that shows which group—creditors or stockholders—has the biggest stake in or the most control of a company:

$$\frac{\text{Total liabilities}}{\text{Stockholders' equity}}$$

RATIO OF NET INCOME TO NET SALES. A ratio that shows how much net income (profit) a company made on each dollar of net sales. Here's the formula:

$$\frac{\text{Net income}}{\text{Net sales}}$$

RATIO OF NET SALES TO NET INCOME. A ratio that shows how much a company had to collect in net sales to make a dollar of profit. Figure it this way:

$$\frac{\text{Net sales}}{\text{Net income}}$$

RETAINED EARNINGS. Profits a company plowed back into the business over the years. Last January's retained earnings, plus the net income or profit that a company made this year (which is calculated on the income statement), minus dividends paid out, equals the retained earnings balance on the balance sheet date.

RETURN ON INVESTMENT (ROI). In its most basic form, the rate of return equals net income divided by the amount of money invested. It can be applied to a particular product or piece of equipment, or to a business as a whole.

SALVAGE VALUE. The amount management estimates a piece of equipment will be worth at the end of its useful life, either as a trade-in or if it were sold for scrap.

SELLING EXPENSES. What was spent to run the sales part of a company, such as sales salaries, travel, meals, and lodging for sales-people, and advertising.

SPECIFIC INVOICE PRICES. An inventory valuation method in which a company values the items in its ending inventory based on the specific invoices on which they were bought.

STOCK. Certificates that signify ownership in a corporation. A share of stock represents a claim on a portion of the company's assets.

STOCKHOLDERS' (OR OWNERS') EQUITY. The value of the owners' interests in a company.

STRAIGHT-LINE DEPRECIATION. A depreciation method that depreciates an asset the same amount for each year of its esti-mated life.

SUM-OF-THE-YEARS' DIGITS. An accelerated depreciation method that makes the sum of the digits in an asset's expected life the denominator for a series of yearly depreciation fractions. The numerators of these fractions are the asset's years of life in reverse order. An increasingly smaller depreciation fraction is applied to the asset's (cost–salvage) value each year.

UNITS OF PRODUCTION. A depreciation method that relates a machine's depreciation to the number of units it makes each accounting period. The method requires that someone record the machine's output each year.

VARIABLE EXPENSES. Those that vary with the amount of goods you produce or sell. These may include utility bills, labor, etc.

VERTICAL ANALYSIS. A financial analysis technique that relates key amounts on the income statement and balance sheet to a 100 percent or base figure for the present and previous year. It shows the percentage change from last year to this year, making it easier to spot problems that require analysis.

WEIGHTED AVERAGE. An inventory valuation method that calculates a weighted average cost per unit for all the goods available for sale. Multiplying that figure by the total units in ending inventory gives you the inventory's value.

Index